HOW TO WORK IN RETAIL

In this Series

Other titles in preparation

WORK IN RETAIL

Practical skills for job applicants and trainees

Sylvia Lichfield and Christine Hall

How To Books

Also by Christine Hall:

How to be a freelance journalist
How to get a job in Germany
How to live and work in Germany
Living and working in China
How to live and work in Britain

Cartoons by Mike Flanagan

British Library Cataloguing in Publication Data
A catalogue record for this book is available from the British Library.

First published in 1996 by How To Books Ltd, Plymbridge House,
Estover Road, Plymouth PL6 7PZ, United Kingdom.

Note: The material contained in this book is set out in good faith for general guidance
and no liability can be accepted for loss or expenses incurred as a result of relying in
particular circumstances on statements made in the book. The laws and regulations are
complex and liable to change, and readers should check the current position with the
relevant authorities before making personal arrangements.

Produced for How To Books by Deer Park Productions.
Typeset by Palimpsest Book Production Ltd, Polmont, Stirlingshire.
Printed and bound by The Cromwell Press Ltd, Broughton Gifford,
Melksham, Wiltshire.

Contents

List of Illustrations

Foreword

Selecting a job or career is never an easy task, many people get it wrong and either move on quickly or spend a period of time being unhappy.

Often the choice is made more difficult because information about the job/career is limited or worse yet, non-existent! Sometimes the advisors are able to provide the basic information such as what qualifications or experience you will need, but they may not be able to explain what the work actually involves.

It is extremely difficult (some would say impossible) to give a real flavourof what the work/industry is like unless you have experienced it. This is clearly why increasingly industrialists are invited to schools and universities to talk to students about their world of work. They can provide a full and colourful picture, and they can answer the questions and queries.

We are not all lucky enough to have access to such opportunities, and often we need to rely upon the written word to provide the information and detail we need about a job.

There is no question in my mind that it is even more difficult to provide the necessary detail in the written form.

However, in the pages which follow is a wealth of information about work in the retail industry. It is not presented as a series of bland facts, but it describes fully the tasks you will actually need to carry out. It gives hints about finding the right type of job for you! It also provides points for discussion, or perhaps just to think about.

The authors, because of their own personal experience of retailing and writing have been able to produce a very readable and informative book.

If you are considering working in retailing, whether you are 16 or 55 I recommend it to you.

Denise Taylor
Operations Manager
Distributive Occupational Standards Council

Preface

The retail sector is one of the biggest areas of employment in the UK, and one of the fields which offers most scope and variety for a career. This book will help you to find your first job and plan your career in retailing.

It will also teach you all the skills you need for a retail qualification at NVQ level 2. You can use it as a textbook or as a self-study course. Supervisors in charge of trainees can use it as a structured programme to complement the in-house training.

At the end of each chapter, you will meet three retail trainees, people like you:

Rebecca Smith is an ambitious eighteen-year-old, set for a career in retail management. Her first job after college is with Streetwise, a fashion boutique in a small town. Rebecca's training progresses well, but the boutique is suffering several blows, including the competition from a new superstore.

John Anderson spent a year travelling around the world, then took a job in a record shop because he didn't know what else to do. He has a laid-back attitude but begins to realise that with training and determination he could get promotion, a better salary, and more job satisfaction.

Linda Cooke, 35, a housewife and mother-of-two, wants to return to work. She hopes to move into a career gradually, beginning with part-time work. Later, when the children are more independent, she plans to work full-time. In the past, she has worked two mornings per week as a volunteer in a charity shop and enjoyed the varied work. Now she applies for a part-time job with Westmore's, a big supermarket which is part of a superstore complex outside the town.

Take some time to complete the assignments ('Points for Discussion') at the end of each chapter. For many of the problems, there is more than one solution. Write down what you would do, how and why. Discuss your results with your supervisor or manager. Your NVQ assessor may also want to see them to assess what you have learnt.

A test at the end of the book will assess if you have the potential to become a good manager. For best results, don't look at the test assignments until you have completed the book and most of your training.

We wish you much success and enjoyment in your training and your future career. If you have any suggestions or comments about this book, we would be pleased to hear from you. Write to us c/o How To Books Ltd, Plymbridge House, Estover Rd, Plymouth PL6 7PZ.

We would like to take the opportunity to thank Dave Brookes of Hindsight Consultancy Service, who put the authors in touch with each other. Many thanks, too, to the retail managers and staff who contributed their comments and experiences which form the basis of our fictional case studies. Mauro V. Corvasce's and Joseph R. Paglino's book *Modus Operandi* was a useful guide in our research for the chapter on preventing theft. For some of the illustrations, we used PageMaker 4 and CorelDraw clipart.

Sylvia Lichfield
Christine Hall

IS THIS YOU?

Presentable   Ambitious

Likes people

Diplomatic   Calm

Organised and orderly

Courteous   Decisive

Likes to achieve targets

Friendly   Alert

Copes with routine tasks

Helpful   Patient

Can use initiative

Discreet   Observant

Efficient

Good listener   Loyal

Can deal with figures

Smart   Thrifty

Good administrator

Responsible   Hygiene conscious

Cool in a crisis

Punctual   Adaptable

Practical

Honest   Reliable

Ready for a challenge

Good communicator   Good manager

1
Finding a Job

Retailing can offer many opportunities as a career. It does not necessarily need the qualities of extreme strength, academic achievement, or youth. There are equal opportunities for both male and female. The aspirations of the employee can be fulfilled, whether it is the need to have a Saturday job whilst at college, an opportunity to earn a little extra cash for a married woman with children, or the desire for a worthwhile, secure and steady job or a high-flying career with long-term benefits.

The basic requirements will be numeracy and literacy but most important will be your interpersonal skills. Do you like dealing with people? Can you remain calm and patient when someone you are dealing with is angry or upset? These are qualities which will provide an excellent service to the customer and a very high degree of job satisfaction to you.

Good customer service is fundamental to the process of retailing. Even if you choose retailing as a career and rise to the more senior management positions, you will never lose sight of the need for customer service in its many forms.

GETTING INTO RETAIL

You may have decided that you want to have a worthwhile, interesting job which is local and will provide you with the necessary income. Alternatively, you may have decided you want a long-term career with promotional prospects and you are prepared to move around in order to achieve your personal goals. So let's deal with these as separate issues.

Working locally

If you are fortunate enough to have a choice of work-places you will need to think carefully about what it is that you want. For example, you may find it more appealing to work in a fashion shop, a specialist motor-spares dealer or a record shop because the merchandise is more interesting to you. If this is the case, do you have some existing knowledge or expertise? If you choose the fashion shop, is the potential customer similar to yourself in relation to age, size, style *etc.* You will feel more comfortable and be able to provide a better service to customers who have similar needs to your own.

You may decide to work in the local supermarket. This can offer working hours which fit in with family commitments and different types of work within the store. You may wish to work on the checkout tills in which case the qualities you need are numeracy and the ability to concentrate over a period of time. Alternatively, you may wish to work on the serving counters such as the delicatessen where personal service is more important to the customer. Finally, you may want to stack shelves. This may require an element of strength and stamina and satisfaction in achieving a tidy and well-presented environment but will not require decision-making or administration skills. So your first task is to decide what is right for you and also, what will be achievable.

The types of jobs we have identified here are usually advertised locally either in the relevant shop window or at the local Jobcentre. There will obviously be more opportunities available at peak times such as Christmas.

An important factor to remember as a job-hunter, is that when a sales assistant leaves a job they will normally only have to give a week's notice. Therefore you may have been making enquiries last week without success but do not be put off making enquiries again this week. If a vacancy has occurred in the last few days, the person who is in the right place at the right time will be the lucky one. Try to make sure it is you!

To increase your chances of finding work locally, it will be advantageous to write to those shops or stores which you have decided you would like to work in and for which you have the necessary skills or qualifications. (See later in this chapter the section on qualifications.) Whilst there may not be a vacancy at the present time, Managers will keep on file those applications which look good and they will save themselves time and money by contacting prospective applicants when a vacancy occurs. Figures 2 and 3 are examples of letters of enquiry which, even though there may be no immediate vacancies, look interesting enough to be kept on file.

Starting a career in retailing

You may have had a Saturday or part-time job in a shop, which may have influenced you in your choice of career. You will now realise that retail management involves stock control, achieving sales targets, managing

```
                                           25 Postmill Street
Mr Gregory                                      St Albans
Off The Record                                     Herts
16 High Street                                  AL88 4DD
Grantwich                                  29th July 19XX
Herts
GR1 4BZ


Dear Mr Gregory


re Full-time sales assistant


I would be very pleased if you would consider my application
for the post advertised in the Grantwich Advertiser.


Having just finished a year gaining experience of world travel,
I decided that I would like a career in retailing. My qualifi-
cations are as follows:-
     GCSE              English              Grade B
                       Maths                Grade B
                       Technical drawing    Grade A
                       French               Grade C
                       Geography            Grade C
     Work experience   I have enjoyed working in various shops
                       and bars in order to support myself whilst
                       travelling the world. During that time I
                       have been involved in filling-up stock,
                       dealing with deliveries and serving
                       customers.
     Interests         Socialising, football.


I feel that I have the necessary experience to fill the post
you are offering and would be very pleased if you would like to
see me for an interview to discuss this further.


Thank you very much for your time in considering this letter.


Yours sincerely



John Anderson
```

Fig. 1. Application letter in response to a local advertisement for a full-time post.

```
                                              Rose Cottage
                                           Highworth Lane
                                               Godalming
Trendsetters                                      Surrey
24 High Street                                 GN27 4TY
Bridgenorth
Surrey                                    4th July 19XX

Dear Madam


I shall soon be starting at the local sixth form
college and would be very pleased if you would consider
me for a job as a Saturday Sales assistant. I would
also be able to work additional hours during the
holidays if you would like me to.


Whilst at school I have been studying for my GCSEs and
am waiting for the results. I have been involved in
various sports activities and have played in netball
matches against other local schools. My other interest
at school has been in the drama club and I have been in
presentations of short plays and I was also in the
fifth-form revue.


I like meeting people and also would like to work in a
fashion shop. If you would like me to come to the shop
for an interview I would be pleased to do so.


Yours faithfully



Tracy Jones
```

Fig. 2. Application for a Saturday job.

42 Dunmow Drive
Middleton
Durham
DU7 4XY

20th October 19XX

Westmore's Supermarket
The New Retail Park
Middleton
Durham

Dear Mr Knight

I have not been working for some time but now that my children are both at school, I would like to return to work.

I have previously done shop work and in my last job I was able to work the till and deal with different payments and vouchers.

I would like to be considered for the evening shift so that my husband can look after the children but I will be able to work Saturdays and possibly bank holidays too.

I hope that you have some vacancies at the moment and I am enclosing a stamped addressed envelope for your convenience.

Yours sincerely

Linda Cooke

Fig. 3. Application letter for a part-time job.

people, staff training, decision-making, time management, budgetary control, wage control and administration. A demanding and satisfying career far removed from the perceived image of 'working in a shop'.

If you really want to get into retail management, you will need to contact major retailing chains who offer management schemes. (See the section on useful addresses at the end of the book.) These fast-track schemes are usually aimed at 'A' level students and preference is given to those who have had some retail experience. If you respond to a national press advertisement for one of these posts you will need a letter, well-composed and presented, and an accompanying CV.

The successful applicant

If your application is successful, you may be invited to an assessment centre where you will take part in a variety of activities. These depend on the organisation involved but may include a one-to-one interview with a senior manager, aptitude tests, numeracy and literacy tests, group discussions (observed by an assessor to identify interpersonal skills), giving a short presentation (to identify confidence and articulation) and/or a problem-solving activity.

Intake for these management trainee schemes is, in most cases, once a year and the programme will include an induction followed by work experience in a variety of shops, providing a programme of different learning opportunities. A trainee will attend courses, together with others who started at the same time, which will cover management skills and company procedures.

You will find that as a trainee manager you will be given support and guidance to help you to achieve success. Most management schemes such as this will aim for an agreed and achievable target which may be (say) to be an assistant manager of a medium store in 18 months.

SPECIALISING

Other specialist activities which are part of retailing but separate from the customer-focused shop or store, may appeal to you. These roles may include buying, merchandising, display and stock control. Selection of candidates for these areas is usually aimed at graduates and there is often a fast-track training programme in the same way as retail management. Large organisations will provide details of schemes they offer.

```
                                        14 Main Road
                                           Middleton
                                             Surrey
Ms D Cross                                  A13 2ZE
Personnel Department
Streetwise plc
Oxford Street
London
W1D 4SR                             24th July 19XX


Dear Ms Cross


re Advertisement for Trainee Managers


I would like to respond to the advertisement in the
Daily Echo on 22nd July for Trainee Managers.


During the last two years I have been working in a
fashion shop and I have enjoyed it very much. My
manager has taken time to talk to me about career
opportunities in the retail business and I have decided
that this is what I would like to do. I would very much
like to be accepted on a management scheme as this will
help me to receive the necessary training and under-
stand that this will take place in my local branch.


I am enclosing a copy of my CV and would be very
pleased if you would consider my application. If you
would like me to provide more information or to attend
an interview I shall be very pleased to hear from you.


Yours sincerely



Rebecca Smith
```

Fig. 4. Application letter for a place on a trainee management scheme for A
level students.

Curriculum Vitae

Personal details

Rebecca Smith
14 Main Road
Middleton
Surrey
A13 2ZE
Telephone 01234 234567

Education

Sept 1989 – July 1994

Guildford High School
Terrace Road
Guildford
Surrey

Sept 1994 to July 1996

Guildford Sixth Form College
St George's Square
Guildford
Surrey

Examinations

English Language GCSE	Grade A	English Literature GCSE	Grade A
Mathematics GCSE	Grade B	French GCSE	Grade C
Geography GCSE	Grade A	Social studies GCSE	Grade A
Biology GCSE	Grade C	Art GCSE	Grade B
Drama GCSE	Grade A		
English Lit. A level	Grade B	Art A level	Grade B
Geography A level	Grade A	French A level	Grade C

Personal achievements

I was Head girl in the final year at high school. This is an elected post and I had to present reasons to groups of fifth year students why I was the best candidate. My role was to help organise charity events, school plays and also to help the prefects carry out their duties.

As part of my studies for A level Geography, I had to assist with a field trip to Norfolk we were making to carry out some research on wildlife and plant life relative to the Broads. It was my responsibility to organise the travel arrangements for the group of 15 students from various parts of Surrey. Not everyone went by the same route or method of transport but, where necessary, I had to arrange the purchase and distribution of tickets and to communicate the details to those concerned. I also had to make sure that everyone knew the time that they should arrive if they were making their own way there.

I have taken driving lessons and passed my test at the second attempt.

Work experience

For the last two years, I have been working in a women's fashion shop. This has been mainly on Saturdays but also during the holidays. I have been involved with looking after the stock, working on the till and serving customers. More recently I have also been assisting with cash and stock administration.

Interests

I like swimming and I play squash regularly.
I also enjoy the cinema and socialising.
I have had a ski-ing holiday with the school and
would very much like to go again.

Fig. 5. Example of a CV.

Developing your career

Entry into a large retail company can provide a multitude of promotional opportunities. In shop management there will be a progression from deputy manager to manager and from small store to medium store to large store. Then there will be area management and then on to executive and director roles.

It may be that you decide to go into training instead of reaching the dizzy heights of the executive. This will mean a sideways step in the management structure but you will then be involved in the training and development of new managers.

Self-motivation, setting personal goals, achieving targets, taking initiatives for improvement in performance of self and others are all building blocks towards promotion. How far up the ladder do you want to go?

GAINING QUALIFICATIONS

It is now possible to gain a qualification in retailing. National Vocational Qualifications (NVQs) are awarded to people based on how well they do their job. They have to show that they understand both how and why they should be doing the job. This can be achieved at different levels – junior sales assistants, senior sales assistants, department managers and store managers. (See page 144.)

Some people find it very difficult to sit and pass exams – you may be one of them! Nerves sometimes take over and your memory goes blank or however much you revise, the questions they ask are the ones you haven't swotted up on. Because retailing is such a practical skill, being judged on how well you actually do your job makes it much fairer than sitting exams.

NVQs also recognise the fact that one workplace may demand different skills and attitudes than another. For example, the customer service in a very exclusive gentlemen's outfitter would be different to that in an average high street shop. Similarly, in some shops, the sales assistant may be involved in the repair or servicing of goods. It would be unreasonable if you were expected to prove that you could carry out these roles when in fact they did not happen in your own workplace.

So, if you decide that you would like to gain an NVQ there are some things which are common to everyone who works in a shop. These are compulsory – but there are others which are optional. You will have a list to choose from and you will pick one or two that are applicable to the type of shop in which you work. (See page 145.)

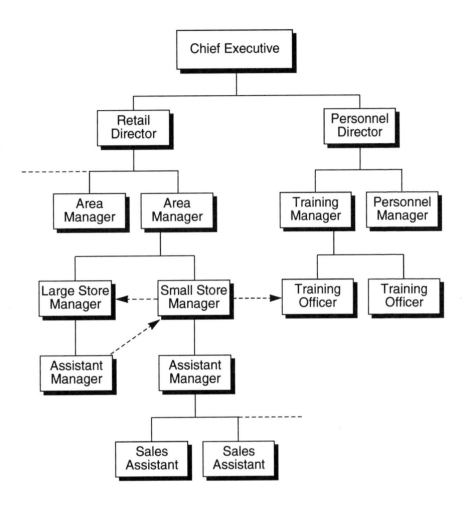

Fig. 6. A typical management structure of a retail company.

The different 'jobs' in an NVQ are called **Units of Competence** and they are broken down into manageable chunks. Let's look at one in particular.

Processing the sale

This is broken down into two parts and the first is entitled 'Operate the payment point'. The standards to aim for include:

- All equipment and relevant materials required on the payment point are available (*bags, vouchers, pens etc*).

- The payment point is opened correctly, at the required time and in accordance with authorised procedures (*before the shop opens*).

- The correct money is placed in the till prior to the commencement of trading (*the float*).

- Change is maintained in the required quantities during trading.

- The cash point contents are made available for authorised collection during operation (*till clears*).

- Customers are informed politely and promptly of any delay in the cash point operation.

- The payment point is closed down in accordance with the authorised procedures.

Some of the words used in the NVQ seem clumsy and not very user-friendly. The words in italics have been added to make them easier to understand.

The NVQ also says that you have to be able to work well, not only during normal trading periods, but also during busy trading periods. This is a further way to prove that a person really can cope under all circumstances.

Also it isn't enough to see that you can do a job correctly but you need to show that you also understand why you are doing it. Your assessor will ask you to explain, for example, what the security procedures are, what happens if mistakes are made and not put right, or what are your company's policies in respect of the operation of the cash point.

The second part of the unit is called 'Take payment for sale'. The standards to aim for include:

- The information is entered into the cash point correctly (details of the sales tag, the price, any credit vouchers *etc*).

- The price/total is stated verbally to the customer.

- The receipt of money/cash equivalent is verbally acknowledged.

- Cheque and credit documents are validated and completed correctly.

- Where situations occur outside own-defined area of responsibility, the appropriate person is called (if unsure, call the supervisor).

- Money/cash equivalents are placed in a secure approved location and the correct procedures followed.

- The correct change is given to the customer.

- Security procedures regarding cash and stock are adhered to (*eg* the till drawer is kept shut except when putting the money in).

- Operator errors are dealt with correctly (*voids*).

- The transaction is carried out in the optimum time (quickly, but not so quickly that errors are made).

- A courteous manner is adopted at all times and the customer is informed of any delay in till operation.

The additional understanding of *why* and *how* procedures are followed will include:

- Knowing which discount vouchers are acceptable.

- How to deal with cheques and credit cards, including authorisation.

- Knowing the legislation regarding under-age purchases and credit transactions.

- Dealing with errors in cheques.

- Knowing when a supervisor should be called.

- Recognising forged bank notes and credit cards and knowing what action to take.

- Using stop lists.

This is an example of one of the 'units' but the others are compiled in a similar way.

ACHIEVING AN NVQ

Because an NVQ is not like an exam where your exam paper is taken away and marked, an assessor will work with you and explain exactly what is involved. They will make an assessment of whether you can do the job properly in several ways – the most frequent is by observation. The trained assessor will watch unobtrusively as the job is being carried out to see if it is being done correctly. In addition, you will have a work book and a file which may include examples of work you have done. In the file you may also have statements from other people who you may have worked with who will corroborate the fact that you are good at your job. And finally, the assessor may ask questions to ensure the understanding of *why* as well as *how* the job is done.

The benefits of achieving an NVQ

One of the benefits of receiving any sort of qualification is the personal pride and sense of achievement. It will be quite hard work and may take as long as eighteen months to get there but at the end you will know that you are really good at your job and have received the correct recognition for it.

If you want to be promoted within your company you will have a tangible record which will be very valuable when you have your staff appraisal.

Because the NVQs are a national award, they are recognised throughout the UK. Therefore, if you should want to move to another company or have to move to another area which means looking for a new job, you will have your certificate which is acceptable to any retail organisation.

If you are in employment your Personnel Department will be able to give you support and guidance regarding registering and assessment for the appropriate level of NVQ.

If, on the other hand, you are seeking employment and want to become a candidate for a National Vocational Qualification your local TEC will give you information regarding colleges and so on which are able to register you for the award. They will also arrange a work placement so that you can gain experience and be assessed in the workplace. (See page 146.)

CASE STUDIES

Now we will see how our three retail trainees set about getting their jobs.
Here we will also meet Tracy, a young friend of Rebecca Smith's, who
inspired by her friend's ambition decides she might like to see whether
working in retail would suit her. Getting a Saturday job is one way to find
out.

Getting a Saturday job

Tracy was starting at the sixth form college in two months' time and she
decided that she would like to earn some extra money for clothes and
socialising. She would also enjoy the work-experience and it would be
good for her CV when she eventually started work.

She went along to the Jobcentre to start with but they had no vacancies
so when she next went shopping in town she decided to try one or two
shops. She had seen an advertisement in the window of the pet shop for
Saturday staff but she didn't fancy that.

What she would really like was to work in somewhere like Trendset-
ters. She bought a lot of her own clothes there, so she would possibly
know some of the customers she would meet.

Tracy decided to go into Streetwise which was another shop that she
liked. She would go in early on Saturday morning before it got too busy.
She knew the manager would not have time to talk to her once the shop
had a lot of customers in it.

'Can I speak to the manager, please?' she asked a sales assistant who
was tidying up the till point. The assistant went to call the manager and
the two came back together.

'I would like to have a Saturday job in a shop like this and I wondered
if you could spare a moment to tell me whether you are likely to have any
vacancies, please,' said Tracy.

'I'm sorry, I have a Saturday assistant at the moment and there is only
one job, except at Christmas. So I can't offer you anything I'm afraid.'

'Would you mind if I give you my details and perhaps you could let me
know if something crops up,' asked Tracy.

'All right. We aren't busy at the moment. Just pop into my office with
me and I'll make a note of your name and so on.'

When they got into the office, Tracy said, 'I often come into this shop
to buy my clothes so I know that I would feel at ease here.'

'Do you like dealing with customers?' asked the manager.

'I can't really say as I haven't worked in a shop before,' said Tracy.
'But I have been involved in organising the school play and I also helped

out in the Mother and Toddler Group as part of my Sixth Form studies. So I have some experience in getting things sorted out and dealing with people who I don't know – and coping with some of the toddlers who were either naughty or upset!'

The manager was busy writing some of these things down. Tracy was feeling pleased that she had gone in when the shop wasn't busy and also that she had felt confident enough to open up the conversation once she had got into the office. The manager had obviously not thought she was being pushy and was being very friendly herself.

Getting a part-time job

Linda Cooke was needing some extra cash now that the two children were at school. There was a never-ending list of things which had to be paid for! There were school trips, special shoes for games, and extra music lessons.

She decided to go along to Westmore's, the supermarket where she always did her shopping, to see if there were any vacancies. When Linda got there she was delighted to see a notice board just inside the door which had vacancies on it. There were a couple for specialist people, a baker and a 'goods inward' person, but more importantly there was a vacancy for a part-time assistant.

Linda read the details carefully and saw that she had to write to the manager. Fortunately, she received an answer by return and went for her interview three days later.

She was feeling a bit nervous but Mr Johnson soon put her at ease. He said that they wanted someone to work on the checkouts between 6 o'clock and 8 o'clock, four evenings a week.

'I don't know how to use these tills you have here,' said Linda. 'I have done till-work before I had the children but I wonder if I would be better at filling the shelves.'

'We will give you the necessary training, so don't worry about it,' said Mr Johnson. They talked for a little while longer and when Linda left, she was not sure whether she should take the job if it were offered. How would she know if she could do it? What if she made mistakes?

Settling down to a steady job

John Anderson had just come back from a year off, travelling round the world. It had been a great experience and he was finding it difficult to get his feet back on the ground.

However, he had to get a job in order to earn some money so he looked in the local press to see what was available. He was lucky to get an interview for the job he wrote for at Off The Record. 'The manager must have liked what I put in the letter,' he thought and began feeling very confident.

John arrived for the interview at exactly the right time 10.00 am − in fact he only just made it! The manager called him in straight away and after the initial introductions asked John why he wanted to work there and what did he think the job entailed. John thought these were pretty stupid questions really. He wanted to earn some money of course and the job was obviously taking money off the customers and putting the records into a bag!

Starting a career in retailing

Rebecca Smith had been working in the local department store at Christmas and during the holidays. She decided that she wanted a career in retail management.

She knew that the Daily Mail was the most likely paper to carry an advertisement in their Retail section for A level students who want to get onto a management course. She wrote for several positions and was delighted when she was invited to attend a one-day selection day. She told Tracy and they agreed to meet and discuss it when she got home.

'How did it go?' asks Tracy.

'Well, it was really nerve-racking, but I think I did OK. There were 20 people altogether and we all had to wait in the foyer before going in to take some written tests. It was a bit like a doctor's surgery but some of us got talking together. That made me feel a bit better. Then we were divided into smaller groups and I had to give a five minute talk on what I liked best at college. Then we had a group discussion on the current problem of providing new motorways and the protests against them. Finally, I had an interview with one of the managers.'

'That sounds like a real ordeal just to get a job!' said Tracy.

'No it wasn't that bad really. And we were all in the same boat. In fact, I really enjoyed the discussions and presentations. I hope that I am going to be lucky. They told us about the job and the training we would receive and it sounds really great.'

POINTS FOR DISCUSSION

1. What was it that Tracy said that improved her chances of being able to work in the shop? What experience had she had that would have improved the likelihood of being given a job as a sales assistant?

2. What experience has Linda had, as a wife and mother, that would also be valuable? There are no clues in the case study so you will have to think for yourself.

3. What experience have you had that may not have been in retailing but would match the skills required to work in a shop?

4. What would you want to ask about the job and training if you were being given that information? What preparation should you carry out before you go for an interview?

5. If you had to give a five minute presentation, what are the important points that would make you appear confident and knowledgeable? nWhat do you think the observers would be looking for when the group was involved in a discussion about the motorway problems?

6. Prepare your own CV showing your qualifications, any work experience with details of your responsibilities and also your personal achievements and interests.

7. What would you wear if you had an interview tomorrow? If you haven't got a suitable outfit, what would you buy?

2
Serving the Customer

The most important person in the shop is always the customer. Give him or her VIP treatment.

Your attitude and service decides whether or not the customers will return to the shop. If they feel irritated by your manners, they will go elsewhere next time. Customers don't have to use your shop; there are plenty of competitors.

THE THREE R's

How do customers decide where to go for their purchases? There are three main factors. They are easy to remember, because all begin with 'R'.

Recognition
The customers recognize the shop front which they have seen before, or the pergola colours which are the same for all branches of your chain, the shop sign, the shop name, or maybe the logo which they have seen in an advertisement.

Reputation
The customers have heard a lot about your shop. In conversations, other people have mentioned that 'Off The Record' is a good place to buy records and CDs.

Recommendation
The customers have asked other people for advice about where to buy a computer, fashionable clothes, CDs or records. Their mates at college have bought CDs at Off The Record and say that the shop has a wide selection; a friend suggests that Street Wise is the most likely place to find a jacket matching the skirt at a reasonable price; a neighbour says that Westmore has the best kept fruit and vegetable section in town.

CREATING A GOOD FIRST IMPRESSION

What makes customers buy? The right item, in the right way, in the right place, at the right price, at the right time. But even if all these are right, something can put the customers off. It is you, the sales assistant.

If they feel ignored or neglected by you, if your manner or clothing irritates them, if they find you pushy or arrogant, they may leave the shop straight away. Perhaps they make their purchase if they really need the item now, but they may not return for more shopping.

The typical customers will decide whether or not the shop and the staff are right within the first moments of being there. First impressions are important, and you have only one chance to create a good first impression.

The following criteria influence the customer's impression:

- attitude
- appearance
- ability

An example of how *not* to do it

Sales assistant: 'Good morning. What are you looking for?'

Customer: 'Eh . . . I think I need a computer.'

Sales assistant: 'What exactly do you need? A PC or an Apple Mac? How many megabyte do you need? Do you want one with a CD Rom Drive? With a dot matrix, an inkjet or a laser?'

Customer: 'I don't really know.'

Sales assistant: 'I see. But surely you know what you need?'

Customer: 'I think I need a computer for my home office, but I don't know anything about computers.'

Sales assistant : 'One would expect that everyone nowadays knows at least the basics about computing . . .'

Then the sales assistant continues in a condescending, patronising tone. What do you think the customer will do? Spend £2000 on a computer in this shop? Unlikely. He or she will visit another shop, or even buy through mail order.

As a sales assistant, your role is to make the customer *want* to buy from your shop.

Your appearance counts

Customers like sales staff who are easily identifiable as shop personnel, for example, wearing a uniform or a name badge. This makes it easy for the customers to approach the right person.

They also expect staff to be smartly dressed and well-groomed. With smart clothing and grooming, you show respect for the customer. What exactly you should wear depends on the shop in which you are working, on the items you sell and the age, wealth and attitudes of your typical customer.

For example, a shop which sells expensive jewellery requires more formal clothing than one which sells garden tools. If you work in a health food and 'fair trade third-world' shop it is appropriate to wear unbleached, embroidered shirts made by a workers' cooperative in India. But the same outfit would be out of place in a shop which sells formal evening wear.

If your shop does not provide a uniform, model your style of clothing on your colleagues.

Looking smart

Before you go to work, and once or twice during the day, check if your appearance is smart. Check the following:

1. Is your hair washed, brushed and tidy?

2. Is there any hair or dandruff on your clothing?

3. Are your clothes clean and ironed?

4. Are there any stains on your tie (especially after lunch)?

5. Are there any make-up or sweat stains on the collar?

6. Are your tights/stockings laddered?

7. Do you smell sweaty, especially the armpits?

8. Are your hands and nails clean?

9. Are your shoes clean (especially after you've been out for a walk during your break)?

10. Do you have noticeable perspiration?

Personal hygiene
You may not notice your own body odour, or the dandruff on the back of your jacket. Colleagues are often too embarrassed to point out that you

have a problem. They may talk about 'methods of airing clothes' or 'effectiveness of deodorants' in general and vague terms, hoping that you'll get the hint.

Avoiding body odour is particularly important in your job, where you are in close contact with customers. Have a bath or shower every day. Change your underwear and shirt or blouse daily and use a deodorant twice a day.

Some people sweat more than others. You may notice that your perspiration is stronger in certain situations, for example when you are under stress or nervous, during your monthly period, or during and after manual work.

It's a good idea to keep a change of underwear, a fresh shirt or blouse, a pair of socks, a deodorant and a flannel at the workplace, just in case you get sweaty and need to freshen up. A spare pair of stockings or tights is also useful in case of 'ladders'.

Using body language

You may not be aware of sending non-verbal messages – called **body language** – and your customers may not be aware of receiving them. But subconsiously they get the message.

You can learn to use body language to give the signals you want to give. Here are the two most effective ways:

1. Smile at your customer

When a customer enters a shop, he or she wants to be noticed. Just a friendly smile, and perhaps a nod from a distance shows: 'I've noticed you. You're welcome in the shop. I am friendly.'

Smiling is easy, and it can make all the difference about how a customer feels about the shop. If you find it difficult to concentrate on your body language, simply remember the smile, and you will achieve a lot.

2. Make eye contact

Look at the customer's eyes when you are talking to them. This says: 'I am interested in you and what you are saying. I have nothing to hide, I am an honest person.'

APPROACHING THE CUSTOMER

Do you speak to the customers as soon as they enter the shop? Or do you give them some time to browse? This depends on the type of shop.

In record and fashion shops, customers usually want to look around on their own first. They may feel threatened if you ask them what they want as soon as they come through the door. Just nod and smile from a distance to make them feel noticed and welcome.

In other shops where goods are 'invisible' or look alike, such as computer shops, customers prefer to be asked straight away.

Your shop probably has its own guidelines on when and how to approach a customer. 'Good morning' and 'good afternoon' are always appropriate. Depending on the type of shop, you can add 'madam' or 'sir'.

Don't ask: 'Can I help you?' The customer will probably answer: 'I don't know if you can.'

It is better to ask: 'How can I help you?' or 'How may I help you?' which sounds more confident and gets to the point quicker.

Some customers who browse are only too shy to ask for your assistance. Disguised calls for help are:

- comparing two products for a long time
- looking around the shop repeatedly.

You should also approach a customer with a friendly 'May I help you?' if they are putting themselves, other customers, or the goods at risk.

Examples

A ten-year-old is looking at the cornflakes packets on the upper shelf at Westmore's Supermarket. She cannot reach them easily. Offer your help, take the goods down from the shelf, and, if necessary, put them back.

A parent with a pram enters the premises of Off The Record. It's a busy Saturday morning, and she tries to manoeuvre the pram between the narrow crowded aisles. Suggest that she leaves the pram in your care near the cash till, or offer to bring her the records she wants to see.

Can you help me please?

Some customers will approach you with a request before you have had the chance to greet them first. Here are examples of how to respond:

1. Customer at Westmore's Supermarket (to assistant Linda who is filling a shelf): 'Excuse me, can you spare me a moment please?'
Assistant Linda: 'Certainly, sir. What can I do for you?'

2. Customer at Westmore's Supermarket: 'Do you sell pet food for guinea pigs?'
Assistant Linda: 'I'm afraid not, madam. But there's a pet shop, three hundred yards up the high street, they should be able to help you.'

3. Customer at Off The Record: 'Where do you keep the CDs of classical operas?'
Assistant John: 'Upstairs, madam, just below the window. Do you need any help?'

4. Customer at Off The Record: 'I'm looking for tapes with music for belly dancing. Do you sell any?'
Assistant John: 'Certainly, madam. We have Egyptian and Turkish belly dance tapes. They're on the first floor. If you go up these stairs, they're on your right, in the folk music section.'

How to respond when you're busy

It can be difficult if you are approached by a customer while you are busy, especially if you are serving another customer.

Examples

1. Customer A (to assistant Linda at Westmore's Supermarket, who is serving customer B): 'Excuse me, I'm in a terrible hurry, I have to catch a train. Do you sell any dry German wine at all? I can't find any.'
   Assistant Linda (to customer B): 'Can you please excuse me, while I show this gentleman where to go. I'll be back in a moment.'
   (to customer A): 'If you come with me. Here are the German wines. The dry ones are on the upper shelf.'
   (to customer B). 'Sorry about that, thanks for waiting. These cooking apples . . .'

2. Customer in wheelchair. 'Excuse me, can you please help me get the apples? I can't reach them on my own.'
   Sales assistant Linda, who is busy clearing and cleaning the floor where a lemonade bottle has been smashed: 'Yes, certainly, sir. Just a moment, while I clear this away and wash my hands. I'll be with you in a moment.'

FINDING OUT WHAT THE CUSTOMER WANTS

Have you ever been on an expedition to buy something and you are not really sure what it is you want?

You go into your favourite clothes shop and there is so much to choose from. Everything you look at is very attractive and you become more and more confused. If only you could buy everything and then there wouldn't be a problem!

A good sales assistant is able to help us in this situation. By asking the right questions, they are able to help us to get a clearer picture of exactly what it is we want so we can make the right decision.

Pointing out the benefits

We make a purchase when the item has a **benefit**. Without being aware of it, we are asking ourselves: 'What will it do for me?'

Some benefits may be:

- it is comfortable
- it does not need ironing
- it makes me look good
- it will last a long time
- it will impress my friends
- it will not crease
- it is cool
- it is warm
- it will be suitable for a casual occasion
- it is good value
- it is the latest trend in fashion
- it's a classic style which won't date.

Earlier in this chapter we looked at approaching the customer at the right time. They may have had time to browse, or they may appear to need some assistance from you.

So you have established a friendly rapport with the customer and now you are ready to offer your expertise.

It is a good idea to ask a question which is related to the possible benefit that the customer is looking for. For example: 'Did you want a particular style or colour?' or 'Did you want something for everyday or were you looking for something a bit special?'

If the question is asked in a courteous and friendly manner, you will find that the customer will be pleased to confide in you and give you some information which will help to know how you can be really helpful.

RESPONDING TO REQUIREMENTS

When you have had some time to find out what the customer wants, you will be able to show how professional you are, and use your stock knowledge. This will enable you to provide a choice of two or three items which will meet the customer's requirements.

Looking at the features

The previous section has provided us with a list of benefits. But all garments and other goods have their own **features** which satisfy those benefits. A feature is something you can see or feel – a benefit is the result! Figure 7 illustrates the relationship between features and benefits.

FEATURE	BENEFIT
'This blouse is cotton . . .	. . . and is cool to wear'
'This shirt is made of polyester . . .	. . . and is non-iron'
'This skirt is lined . . .	. . . and will not crease or ride up'
'These shoes are wide fitting . . .	. . . and will be comfortable'
'This wine is sweet . . .	. . . and goes well with Chinese food . . .'
'This salad mix is ready washed . . .	. . . and you can eat it immediately'
'This CD has music in twelve different ballroom dance rhythms . . .	. . . and you can use it to practise your ballroom dancing'
'This carpet has a bold pattern . . .	. . . and can take a lot of wear'
'This carpet is brown and grey . . .	. . . and you don't have to vacuum it often'

Fig. 7. A list of features and benefits.

Knowing about the stock which is available in your store and being able to understand the features and benefits will help you match the customer's requirements.

In addition, it is important to know where stock is displayed, whether it is available, or if it can be ordered if it is currently out of stock.

CLOSING THE SALE

Achieving a sale is the main objective of a sales assistant's job.

The customer will be leaving the store with an item which exactly suits their needs and the store will be nearer to meeting the sales targets. A win/win situation! When this happens, the customer will come back time and time again.

But what sometimes goes wrong? Why does the sales assistant sometimes find it difficult to close the sale?

What goes wrong?

When a customer is anxious for advice or guidance regarding an item, and whether it is exactly what they want, it is essential that the response from the sales assistant is honest.

To give misinformation or to say that a garment looks good when it really does not, serves no purpose whatsoever. The customer may buy the item but the results are short term, and may have a longer lasting detrimental effect. The least amount of damage that can come out of this transaction is that the item will come back for a refund when the customer realises that it is not what they wanted.

More likely, they will never come back to the store again. So potential future sales are lost from that customer and there is data to prove that customers tell all their friends whenever they receive bad service.

Why sales assistants cannot close the sale

There is a misconception that 'selling' is trying to get someone to buy something they do not want.

Consider instead, how you will be assisting your customer when they are confused and uncertain.

You will ask them what they need (the benefit they are looking for). You will be able to identify the item with the feature that will provide that benefit. This is your expertise. You are the professional. A customer will not know about everything in the store, but you will!

In order to close the sale, you restate the points that you have discussed in your conversation. For example: 'I know that you said comfort is important. Which of these two is the most comfortable?' or 'This is the style which is the latest fashion trend, and just right for the party you are going to.'

By this method, you will confirm what the customer wanted and why. Also that the item in question is exactly what they want.

COPING WITH DIFFICULT SITUATIONS

Meeting the angry customer

Difficult situations often arise when a customer is angry. It may not be your or your shop's fault. Sometimes they are angry before they enter the shop. They may have quarrelled with their husband or wife, or been told off by their boss.

But sometimes customers are angry because something went wrong in the shop: they could not get the right product or information, or feel neglected.

The rules for treating angry customers are the same, whatever the cause of their anger: You must try to stay calm, friendly and polite. Listen to what they say. Avoid contradicting them or accusing them of anything. Remember that the customer – even one who behaves unreasonably – is the most important person in the shop. Try to make them leave the shop with positive feelings. It is easy to turn an angry customer into an ex-customer.

Helping a shy customer

Many customers feel embarrassed in a shop. If you are aware what embarrasses them, you can adopt the right attitudes to make them feel more at ease.

Customers can get embarrassed because of the following reasons:

1. They don't know much about the product they want (for example, a computer) and are afraid of asking for help, for fear that they'll appear stupid.

2. The layout of the shop is unfamiliar, and they feel lost.

3. The goods cost far more than they can afford, or the price labels are not visible.

4. The type of product embarrasses them, especially if it is a personal item and they are buying it for the first time. Think of the woman who buys a packet of condoms for the first time, the teenager getting her first bra, or the man who is buying tampons for his wife.

5. The sales assistant's attitude upsets them. Think of the perfectly mani-cured, heavenly beautiful sales assistant in the cosmetics shop who makes the casually dressed, unmade-up housewife and mother-of-four feel clumsy and ugly. Or remember the patronising sales assistant in the computer shop who talks jargon the customer doesn't understand.

Keeping a diary
Record all difficult situations with customers. Write down:

1. What was the cause of the problem?

2. How did you resolve it?

3. What was the result?

4. Was the customer satisfied at the end?

5. If the same situation occurred again, what would you do differently?

Item number five is the most important one. Everyone makes mistakes. What counts is what you learn from them.

CASE STUDIES

John thinks about his image
John has worked at the same branch of Off The Record for some time. When a vacancy for assistant manager comes up at another branch, he asks his manager, Mr Gregory, to recommend him.

Mr Gregory hesitates. 'You certainly have the experience, you know the world of music inside out, you get on well with young customers. You are an excellent sales assistant, but I'm afraid you don't have the personality for an assistant manager.'

John asks what exactly Mr Gregory means. 'They are looking for some-one who is more mature, who has the right image for an assistant manager, and who has the right attitude to all customers, not just the young ones.'

For a while, John doesn't think about the matter any more. But then he learns that the new assistant manager is younger than he, and has less experience. So it is not just age and experience which shape a person's image. He starts thinking.

Rebecca serves a customer

Rebecca is busy tidying the skirts so that they look attractive when she notices a customer who is holding up two skirts for a closer look and has a puzzled expression on her face.

She decides to offer some assistance, so she approaches the customer with a smile and says: 'Are you finding it difficult to make up your mind?'

'Yes. I just can't decide which one I ought to buy,' replies the customer.

Rebecca tries to find out what the problem is. 'Do you want the skirt for a special occasion, or is it the style you are unsure of?'

'What I want is something comfortable for work that I can wear frequently, without having to spend too much on dry-cleaning bills.'

Rebecca looks at both skirts. 'The one with the soft pleats is a very comfortable style. Let's look at the label to find out how it should be cared for.'

It is exactly what the customer wants: The symbols on the label show that it can be machine-washed and dried in the tumble dryer.

'There you are,' Rebecca says. 'Comfortable for sitting in the office and you can put it in the washing machine as often as you like.'

'Thank you very much,' the pleased customer says. 'You have been very helpful. I may have chosen the wrong one and regretted it later.'

Linda meets an angry man

Linda notices a man stamping up and down the aisles at Westmore's supermarket. 'Can I help you?'

'I don't think anyone can. Not in this b. . .y place. You never have anything I need.'

Linda has worked at Westmore's for only a month, but she knows that the man is not right.

'That's not true,' she protests. 'Only last week we had those funny cereals you wanted, and you remember it well.'

The customer goes red in the face. 'What business is that of yours?' His shouting attracts other customers who gather curiously.

Linda feels she cannot let him treat her like this. 'You started by claiming we never have anything you want. It's just not true. Don't make such claims.'

She notices his flushed face, and his breath smells of alcohol. She looks at the contents of his shopping basket: a selection of gin, whisky and beer. 'And I'm not talking to drunks.'

The customer slams his shopping basket on the floor. The gin and whisky bottles in it break, the drinks spill on the floor. The customer stamps out of the store.

The supermarket manager, alerted by the loud voices, comes out of his office. He looks at the crowd of customers in the aisles, at the mess on the floor, and finally Linda.

'Please clear this away at once. And then come to my office, please, Linda.'

For the first time, it occurs to Linda that she might get the blame for the incident.

POINTS FOR DISCUSSION

1. John wants to make sure he is in line for promotion when another opportunity comes up. He realizes he has to change his image. How do you think an assistant branch manager of a record shop should dress? Are there any differences between the dress codes of sales assistants and managerial staff? Does Mr Gregory's comment contain any other hints on how John can improve his image?

2. You are assistant manager at a branch of Off The Record Ltd. The shops sell LPs, singles, music cassettes and CDs. Business is growing, and the company has taken on new staff who are uncertain what to wear. Your manager asks you to draft clothing guidelines for the sales staff. He asks you to consider the following:

   − The new recruits have retail experience in other fields. One worked in a supermarket where uniforms were provided, one in a garden centre where jeans were appropriate, and one in an art gallery where she wore a black suit with short skirt and high heels all day.

   − Off The Record has no staff uniforms, but would consider introducing them if there was a real advantage.

   − Staff at Off The Record Ltd are male and female, aged 18 − 65, but most are in their twenties.

– Selling records and CDs does not involve dirty, manual work, but occasionally staff are asked to help with some dusting or cleaning a shop window.

– The shop is arranged on two floors. Pop, rock, punk, rap and the current top ten hits are on the ground floor. Upstairs is a smaller room with a classical and a folk music section.

– The shop has a larger punk and 70s music selections than any other shop in the area; in fact, 60 per cent of the turnover comes from 70s rock and punk.

– 50 per cent of all customers are aged 18 – 30; 30 per cent are aged 31 – 45.

– Your manager wants the guidelines to cover details (including shoes, jewellery, name badges, hairstyles, make-up).

3. The customer in case study 2 wanted a garment which was (a) comfortable and (b) easy to care for. Other requirements could be 'for a wedding so it needs to be extra special' or 'a particular length to complement a jacket' or 'cool for a holiday'.
   Next time you buy something – it does not have to be clothing – make a list of as many special features and benefits as possible.

4. Go to a clothes shop. Look critically at least five items and imagine that you are identifying features and benefits for a customer. This may involve looking closely at style, colour, fabric, sew-in care labels or fabric.

5. Look at Linda's case study. She was clearly not prepared for this situation. She took it personally and responded emotionally. If she had anticipated the customer's behaviour, she might have responded differently.
   Look carefully at what she said. In what ways could she have handled the situation better?

6. Remember the most difficult situation with customers you have experienced, something really tricky, embarrassing, or frightening. Analyse it as described under 'Keeping a diary'.
   Imagine how you would respond if the same situation occurred again. Write it down.

3
Displaying and Merchandising Stock

Some companies invest money in different forms of advertising. Advertisements can be placed in any of the different types of media available and can range from simple and inexpensive to highly sophisticated and very costly.

However, the display of goods in any retail outlet is, in fact, a form of advertising. It is a way of making the goods attractive to the customer and enticing them to buy. As customers we are influenced by visual presentation and if a shop, an item, a range of products looks good we immediately want to find out more. Conversely, if it looks dull or uninteresting we will look elsewhere.

WINDOW DISPLAYS

A shop window is a 24 hour advertisement – people window-shop whenever they are walking along the street, even if the shops are closed.

If you are creating a new window display, there are some basic, important rules.

- Empty the window of all existing goods and display equipment.

- Ensure that the floor, walls, and equipment are free of dust, stickers and dirty marks *etc*.

- Check that the display equipment that you will be using is in good condition and safe.

Choose the merchandise that you are going to display. Again there are some basic rules to follow.

- Does the merchandise reflect the current trends or promotions?

- Is it clean and of high quality?

- Does it look good together as a group of items?

- Does the group present a theme or co-ordinated idea?

- Is there too much merchandise which may risk a cluttered look?

Creating the display

The eventual display which you create should be attractive and informative. You will already have been considering how to make it attractive in your choice of merchandise and preparation of a clean and high quality display area. You will need to create the visual effect now and this may need some experimentation to get the best effect. Trying different positions and angles for the merchandise can often present a totally different, and more attractive, result. Stand back and see how it looks before you are sure you are totally satisfied.

Finally, the customer will be wanting information. So make sure that your ticketing is accurate and ideally placed for the customer to read and know which item it refers to.

INTERNAL DISPLAYS

These are similar in concept to the shop window and may have several purposes:

- to promote a particular range of goods
- to guide and entice a customer to a particular department
- to identify a particular event such as a sale or discounted offer.

But the emphasis will be the same – to attract and entice.

MERCHANDISING

Effective merchandising will play a very significant part in achieving sales targets.

The definition of good merchandising is: **Having the right stock, in the right place and in the right proportions.**

'The right stock' could mean any of the following:

• Seasonal – for fashion merchandise or sportswear.

• A response to change, *ie* it may be summer but if there are forecasts of rain, you will lose sales in a clothes shop if you cannot offer an umbrella or lightweight coat.

• A response to current crazes *eg* computer games, football strip.

• It could reflect a current advertising campaign which the public will be aware of.

• It could be following through a theme or topic which is in the window.

'The right place' really means 'where the customer can find it'. If their interest is engaged by a good window, an advertisement, the immediacy of a current trend, they will soon lose interest if they cannot find the goods they are looking for. So, wherever possible, a high-selling item should be at the front of the store or department, whichever is appropriate.

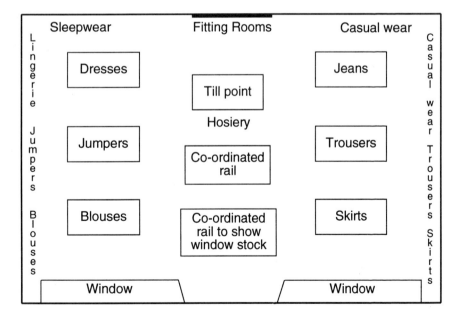

Fig. 8. A typical floor layout in a Streetwise Shop.

A bad retailer will make the mistake of placing a poor selling line at the front of the store in the hope of getting rid of it – seldom does this work! Goods do not sell for the simple reason that the customers do not want them. Don't waste good selling space with poor lines.

If it is not possible to place the stock in a prominent place where it is immediately visible to the customer, you can achieve a similar effect by having banners or posters which are eye-catching and draw the customer to the area of display.

'Having the right stock' is one thing, but 'in the right proportions' is quite another. This is more difficult but can be the successful result of the analysis of sales and stock levels. In simple terms, if a fashion retailer could accurately forecast that they were going to have ten potential customers who would want to buy a particular shirt, it would be important to have ten shirts out on display. If there were only seven on display, then three sales would be lost.

If space is not available for ten shirts, this can be counteracted by constantly refilling shelves in response to sales. Other retail outlets, for example electrical retailers, would not display quantities of items, so they must always make sure that an example is on display and sufficient stock is available in anticipation of other sales.

In order to achieve these results, it is important to have an awareness of sales forecasts and these figures can be based on:

- last year's figures as a comparison
- current stockholding
- trends
- impact of other competitors in the High Street.

SPECIAL PROMOTIONS

Special promotions are a method of increasing sales and usually involve discounted prices.

It is very important that the customer is aware of the new, current selling price and where appropriate, what the original selling price was. This is displayed as an incentive to the customer. Everyone likes a bargain! However, it is essential, in law, that this information is accurate.

Swing tickets, banners and posters are all used to bring to the attention of the customer what is being offered.

CASE STUDIES

Increasing sales through co-ordinated items

Rebecca noticed that the window display had just been completed and was showing a new range of merchandise in the latest autumn colours.

She asked her manager if she could make an internal display to promote the goods and make them more noticeable and attractive inside the shop.

The manager thought it was a good idea and asked Rebecca to carry on and she would have a look at the results later.

The items in the window were skirts, blouses, a dress and jumpers – all in a collection of soft browns and beiges. Inside the shop they were all on display just inside the doorway – all on separate rails.

The first thing that Rebecca decided to do was to put a jumper over the blouse that was at the front of the rail and then she went to the accessory department and found a pair of earrings that co-ordinated beautifully. As soon as she saw them all together Rebecca decided that she would buy all three when she got paid on Saturday!

She clipped the earrings just over the edge of the jumper but it showed them off very well.

Then she went back to the accessory department and this time chose a silk scarf which she knew would look good with the dress. She had already learned that a dress on a hanger does not always look good – she had heard her manager say that it did not have 'hanger-appeal' – and she felt sure that by draping the silk scarf across the shoulder it would make it come 'alive'. She was pleased with the results and considered whether a necklace would make it look even better or whether it might be a bit too much. She decided that the scarf was just perfect on its own.

The type of display equipment that was being used also had the facility to put a large square shelf on top. So Rebecca went and took one from the store-room. She dusted it carefully as it hadn't been used for a while and made sure that all the necessary fixings were in place. Then she attached it carefully to the unit on the shop-floor. She had to be extra careful doing that because the display was already creating some interest and there were customers trying to have a look at the new merchandise. She had to make sure that she did not get in their way or allow any of the equipment or tools to be left in a place where someone might trip over them.

Having placed the shelf securely, Rebecca then put the stock in place. She had chosen a blouse, a skirt and a jumper of a different colour to the one she had put over the blouse already. She draped the skirt so that it hung slightly over the edge of the shelf and then placed the blouse on a small frame and the jumper alongside. She wasn't entirely happy with her efforts at first but by slightly altering the way the blouse hung, she realised it looked great. She then placed the necklace which she hadn't used earlier on top of the folded jumper.

Her manager was really pleased and said that Rebecca could have special responsibility for internal display in future. But what was really good was that on three separate occasions later that day Rebecca saw a sale go through the till which was for two or three items all chosen from her display. One customer even remarked to the sales assistant that she was so pleased to see all the items displayed together like that as she always had a problem choosing things that would look good together and the necklace and earrings were just the finishing touches.

Increasing sales by creating interest

John knew that Catastrophe, the rock group, were performing at the club on the outskirts of town next month.

The had always had a good sale of their records as Catastrophe were frequently in the top 20 list of CDs. This concert was going to boost sales even more.

But there are a lot of record shops in town. John wondered how he could make sure that the additional sales came into the tills of Off The Record and not one of the other record shops.

He had a month before the concert so he decided to write to the promoter of the concert and ask if he could have a large poster-type photograph. He was lucky and they sent two different ones.

A week before the concert was due to take place, John put the two posters in the window and a display of all the CDs that Catastrophe had ever produced. He managed to highlight with bright coloured backgrounds the most recent release and he also included a poster for the concert. He did wonder about that because he seemed to be doing some advertising for someone else's benefit!

However, when he had finished the display, he went and stood on the opposite side of the shopping mall to see how effective it was. He was sure that it was eye-catching and that it would draw the customers in.

Sales of the CDs went up – but then he knew they would anyway because of the concert. What convinced him that some of it was due to his efforts was when at least five customers came in and said, 'Do you sell posters like the ones in the window?'

John had to say, 'No, I'm very sorry they are for display only.'

But the result had been achieved. The customer was buying the records in his shop instead of one of the other record shops in town!

Increasing sales through linked produce

Linda had been for a short break to France and was really impressed with the cheeses and breads she had tried.

When she came back, she was telling her manager about it. 'Can I do a display inside the store?' she asked. 'We had such a wonderful lunch one day and all it was was cheese, bread, grapes and wine. They really went well together but because we have them all separate in the store our customers don't always have the chance to relate them together.'

'No, you're right,' he said. 'I'm sure most people who have been to France will have had a lunch like you have just described. We have just got to remind them and get their taste-buds going!'

Linda could not make a display on the shop floor as the wine would need watching for security reasons and the cheese would have to be displayed where it was cool. So she spoke to the departmental manager on the delicatessen and together they chose an area on top of the counter.

When they had finished, it looked really appetising. There was a bottle of wine, two glasses, some nice fresh grapes, a small selection of cheeses and a baton of bread.

'You've made a good job of that,' said her manager later on when Linda had gone back to the till. 'I have noticed several people comment on it. Do you think you could do that each Saturday morning? I think that is the time when we are most likely to get the best results from your idea. Well done!'

POINTS FOR DISCUSSION

1. How could you use a creative idea to entice and attract customers to buy products which at first glance seem very ordinary *eg* tools, kitchen utensils, stationery *etc* ?

2. If you are going to monitor the effectiveness of your displays to see if they have produced more sales, how can you measure the success in quantifiable results?

3. Produce a report, to discuss with your assessor, on three windows in your own High Street that are:

(a) creative   (b) eye-catching   (c) uninteresting

How would you have approached the last one?

4. Is there a display idea in your store which is going to be affected by time of day or time of week? Can a display be made quickly to capitalise on this?

4
Processing the Sale

When a customer has made a purchase, almost invariably, the last thing they do before they leave the shop is to pay for the item. For this reason, the person who is working on the till-point has a key role. The transaction will be the last thing the customer experiences and will be the memory he or she takes away with them. They may have had bad or indifferent service up to that point, but it can all be put right before they go out of the shop. On the other hand, they may have received excellent service by a colleague who helped them to make a choice or found them exactly what they were looking for. What a pity if it all goes wrong in the last two minutes!

OPERATING THE TILL-POINT

Try to think of situations which have not been entirely to your liking when you were a customer. We don't want to be held up because there is insufficient change in the till or there are not any bags of the right size in which to put the goods. A good sales assistant will think ahead and anticipate the requirements.

Housekeeping is something we shall be dealing with later, but the till-point is the one point where the customer is not looking at the merchandise and has a chance to look at the surroundings. We all make an effort when we are having visitors into our homes to make sure that everywhere looks neat and tidy. The customers are your visitors and will enjoy coming to see you if you create the right environment. So make every effort to keep the till-point tidy. Make a list of the things you will actually need. These may include a pen, a notepad, bags or wrapping paper, credit documents, scissors, a tape measure. It will not include the baby's bonnet that was found in the shop, an assortment of odd coins, two hundred hangers, an empty coffee mug, discarded tickets from merchandise *etc*. Elbowing everything aside in order to make space to write a cheque is going to make a very bad impression. Even the things which are definitely necessary can probably be stored in a drawer and still be easily accessible when required.

It is always a good exercise to stand back and imagine you are a customer. See the till-point through their eyes. How does it look?

Of course there will be times when you are very busy and keeping up appearances is difficult. But like visitors to your home, the customers will understand if the reasons are genuine. And when you are extremely busy and a queue has formed, it only takes a second or two to smile at each customer and to occasionally apologise for keeping them waiting. You don't have to say it to each customer as they will all hear you and will appreciate your courtesy under difficult circumstances. They will actually be on your side and be sympathetic.

INPUT METHODS

Entering transactions may be done in a variety of ways depending on the size of the organisation and the sophistication of the stock-taking technology. On the one hand, there may be a simple cash drawer in a counter. On the other, there may be a till which records the sale, makes a note of the item going out of stock, takes into account sales-trends and requirements and reorders the item if appropriate. The latter of these two is actually a computer and can also provide records of cash and stock at the end of each day's trading.

However, whichever method you experience in your own place of work, there will be a correct way of doing things and you must follow these procedures. Inaccurate recordings of sales transactions will adversely affect the information regarding both cash and stock.

If the cash is recorded incorrectly, a correct reconciliation cannot be carried out at the end of the day. If sales to the value of £1,000 have been rung up but there is only £990 in the till, then the discrepancy has to be accounted for. Was the person operating the till being careless? Or even worse, dishonest? You will not want to give the impression of either of these situations so it is always as well to be very careful when working on the till.

If the stock is recorded incorrectly, an inaccurate picture of trading patterns can be fed into the stock-control mechanisms. As a result, the replacement stock will not be the right stock to meet the potential sales and takings will go down.

TAKING PAYMENTS

Shops and stores offer a variety of payment methods to their customers in order to make it easier for them. It is part of the customer service that is offered. In addition, many stores have their own credit card and this is to encourage customer loyalty.

Whichever method of payment is being made there are some important rules to be followed:

- Be accurate when informing the customer of the total cost.

- Enter the transaction correctly according to company procedure.

- Give the correct change or documentation to the customer.

- Do not have the till drawer open any longer than is necessary.

When the customer offers cash as the payment method, you will find it helpful if you state the value as they hand you the money *eg* 'Thank you. Ten pounds.' This reinforces the amount in your own mind and will help to ensure the correct change is given. It can also overcome the likelihood of a customer claiming that a larger amount was given.

To alleviate any further confusion, it is always beneficial to count the change back to the customer.

Accepting cheques and credit cards

When taking payment by cheque or credit card, there are additional checks which must be made:

- Is the signature correct?

- Is the expiry of the card out of date?

- Is the information correctly completed? Date, words, figures.

- Is the card a forgery? Look for tell-tale signs.

- Is the customer on a stop list?

- Is the floor level exceeded? If so, an authority will be needed from the credit card company.

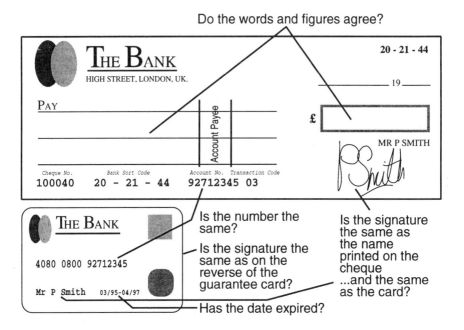

Fig. 9. What to look for when accepting cheques.

The banks and credit card companies lose millions of pounds each year through the misuse of cheques and credit cards. In order to prevent this, there are safeguards built into the production of credit cards and salespeople should be aware of these so that they can look out for them.

Firstly, the strip on the back of a card which is the space for the signature, is a special type of paper which is difficult to reproduce. It will have the name or logo of the bank printed repetitively all over it. Look at your own to see this. If a card falls into the wrong hands or the new 'owner' tries to enter their own signature on to the strip it will be possible for a sharp-eyed sales assistant to detect that it has been tampered with. Sometimes a fluid is used to take off the original name but when the new signature is written on, the writing is fuzzy.

Secondly, the banks have invested a great deal of money in order to put a hologram on the front of the card. This is very difficult to reproduce fraudulently so do check to see that all the cards which you handle have got one. You can test a card by moving it slightly so that the light catches the hologram. It will also be in a logo or design specific to the issuing bank.

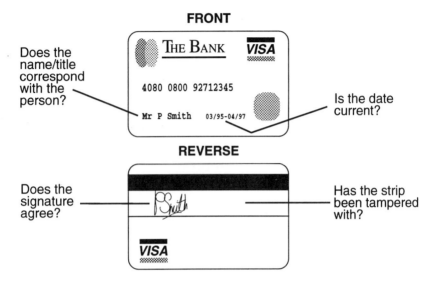

Fig. 10. What to look for when accepting credit cards.

The banks and credit card companies are very anxious to reduce the amount of fraudulent use of cards and offer a reward to sales assistants who identify and withhold a card.

What to do if you suspect attempted fraud

If you think that you have been given such a card, there is a procedure that you must follow.

- Go to the telephone, taking the card with you and call the number of the credit card company. This will be the same number that you will ring if you need an authority code for a purchase which is over the floor limit.

- As this is a situation where you think the card is forged, there will be a code signal which you give to the person who takes the call which will immediately alert a senior member of staff. This is very discreet and will not be understood by customers if your telephone is within earshot of the shopfloor.

- You will be asked a series of questions which only need the answer 'Yes' or 'No'. This is again for discretion and will not offend a customer.

• If you are requested to withhold the card from the customer, leave the card behind and go and give the information to the customer. It is usually sufficient to say that the card has been retained for audit purposes and the customer will be receiving information from the credit card company direct. This will enable you to explain that they did not divulge any further details.

So you see, the person who is working on the till has a great deal of responsibility. They have to offer the highest level of customer service. They have to be 100 per cent accurate in recording the sale *ie* stock and cash. They have to be alert at all times for incorrectly or fraudulently used cheques or credit cards. They have to be able to deal with potentially difficult situations in a calm and efficient manner which will not offend or aggravate customers.

CASE STUDIES

Sales over the floor limit

John was serving a customer who was buying seven CDs and the total price was over the floor limit in Off The Record. As a result, John had to go to the telephone to get an authority code.

He filled in the voucher and put it through the imprinter. Then he said to the customer 'Would you excuse me for a moment. I need to go through another procedure on this sale.'

'What's the problem?' asked the customer with a puzzled look.

'There is no problem. It's just a formality and won't take a moment or two. Sorry to keep you waiting.' He looked at the customer with an open, friendly expression and started moving towards the office where he could make the necessary phone call. He had the card with him and all the details he needed.

He rang the number of the credit card sanctioning department and gave the details. John wasn't concerned that the card was stolen – he was simply following procedures. He had a pen ready to take down the authority code. He knew he would not be able to remember it so with a pen ready, he would be able to write the number down, on the voucher, as it was given to him.

When he got back to the customer, he said, 'Thank you very much. Sorry to have kept you waiting.' He politely gave the voucher, the card, the till receipt and the goods to the customer.

Dealing with cards which may be stolen

It was Tuesday morning and Linda had just been in the staff room with everyone else for staff training. The subject this week was security and apparently there were some stolen credit cards being used in the area.

All the till staff had been given a list which they had to keep discreetly at the till and be aware of what to do if they were presented with a card which was on the list.

It was now 10 am and here was one of the names! Linda knew that she should not show any outward sign of concern or panic but she also knew that she had to deal with the problem.

'I'm sorry but there is a slight problem with the credit card system. I will just call my supervisor. Sorry to keep you waiting.'

'You haven't even tried to put it through the machine,' said the customer angrily.

Even though Linda had given the coded ring, two presses of the button, it still took a moment or two for the supervisor to arrive. By which time the customer was getting even angrier.

'What's wrong with my card. Are you saying I haven't got the money to pay for it?'

'No, of course not. But you will realise that the procedures we have to follow are laid down and I simply carry them out. It does mean that I don't make any decisions or have any knowledge about the customer.' Linda was making sure that she was staying calm and speaking in a level manner.

Fortunately the supervisor came along and the problem was no longer Linda's responsibility.

Using diplomacy in a difficult situation

Rebecca was working on the till and a customer made a purchase with her company credit card. She carefully got the stop list from under the till and had a look at the entry. They were in alphabetical order so it only took a second or two. Had the name not been on the list, she knew that she could have carried on ringing up the sale. But there it was, on the stop list, so she had to go to the telephone and make an authorisation call.

'Sorry about this. I've just got to make a telephone call regarding this card.'

'What's the problem?' asked the customer.

'I really don't know,' said Rebecca. 'Sometimes there are problems with certain numbers on the computer. They never tell us! Just make us do more work!'

Rebecca went to the telephone, went through the procedures, and the person on the other end said that the customer was in arrears and could only make a purchase provided she made another payment of £10 on to her account.

Rebecca was given an authorisation code which could only be used if a payment was made first.

'Is it OK?' said the customer with a worried look.

'Not quite,' said Rebecca with a smile. 'I need you to make a payment of £10 before I can put the sale through. So if you don't mind, can we deal with that first? You can pay by cash or cheque whichever is easier.'

'What do you mean!' said the customer angrily. 'What's wrong with my account!'

Calmly Rebecca replied, 'I can't really help you with that query. The card people don't discuss anything like that with me or give me any details. If you want to know about your account you will have to give them a ring yourself. I'm sure they will be most helpful. In the meantime, all they said to me was that Mrs Smith will be making a payment before this purchase. So I'm just following instructions. I'm sure it can't be anything too serious or they would have told me not to serve you!' she said with a grin.

The customer felt better then and she thought to herself, 'This girl doesn't seem to know that I am in arrears. That would have been really embarrassing!'

POINTS FOR DISCUSSION

1. Should John have told the customer he was over the floor limit? What is the danger of doing this from a security point of view?

2. What did John do that made the process easier and not embarrassing to the customer?

3. How will the supervisor now deal with Linda's problem? If Linda is right and the card is stolen what will be the next course of action?

4. If the customer realises that the staff are well trained and that she has not been able to get away with the fraudulent use of a stolen card, she may just leave the goods and run out of the shop. What is the best course of action then?

5. How can the stop list be consulted in the most discreet way? Where must the list be kept?

6. What would Rebecca have done if the customer was so far in arrears that the sale could not be allowed?

7. What would have been the result to the store if Linda had not been trained or had not been keeping her wits about her and the customer had been able to use the stolen card?

5
Accepting Returns and Complaints

DEALING WITH RETURNS AND EXCHANGES

When a customer returns an item to your shop it may be for one of two reasons. Firstly, it may be that the item is in some way faulty or is not of 'merchantable quality'. This means it is not suitable for the purpose for which it was sold and the customer is legally entitled to a replacement which is in perfect condition. A simple problem may exist, such as a button missing off a garment or a more serious example is a piece of equipment which simply does not work. In cases such as this, the customer does not need a receipt but some identification that the goods may have been bought at your store, for example a sew-in label in a garment, a company bag or an item that is regularly or exclusively sold in your store.

This is a form of complaint and should be dealt with as such. If you help the customer to understand that you are taking care of their problem you will be able to diffuse any anger or dissatisfaction they may have had with the product and your company.

It could also be the case that you do not have a similar item in stock which is in perfect condition – and remember this is what the customer is entitled to. However, if you have established a good relationship with the customer, they may be happy to take a different item instead or a cash refund. We will talk more of that later.

The second reason that the customer may be bringing an item back is simply because they have changed their mind. This is quite different in law and the customer is not entitled to a refund as a right. However, many companies do allow this to happen in the interests of goodwill and the company policy will be made clear to all members of staff. A satisfied customer is one who will come back time and time again and an example of this was demonstrated by a fashion shop who allowed a customer to buy two dresses. The customer wanted a dress for a special occasion and she was unsure which one of two to choose; she did not have the correct shoes on, her make-up was not freshly created and the ordeal was making her feel slightly hot and bothered. The sales assistant suggested that she should take both. She explained that she would have to actually pay for both dresses but would then have the benefit of trying them both on in the comfort of her own home wearing the correct accessories and possibly having a second opinion from the family. The customer was delighted. She knew that she would be given a refund without a problem when she came back the next day and was happy to pay for both in the first instance. And which shop did she go back to next time she wanted a new outfit? It's easy to understand how a really good service, when dealing with refunds, can actually increase business.

There will also be times when you feel that the customer may have been responsible for the fault or damage to the item. This will need a great deal of tact and diplomacy and there may be times when the item can be tested by an independent authority, if a serious claim is made. However, many organisations will only take this course of action in the event of a serious or large problem and will in the interest of goodwill give the benefit of doubt to the customer's claim.

Your own manager will be able to give advice and guidance about the law or any trade legislation regarding the customer's rights.

So you must be sure of the law and of your own company's policies with reference to refunds before taking any action.

COMPENSATING THE CUSTOMER

This can take several forms depending on the reason why the customer is wanting compensation. The most usual of these can be:

- a refund of the total cost of the item

- a replacement item

- a refund of part of the cost if the item is faulty or damaged

- a cash offer to pay for cleaning if the item is marked or dirty

- a repair of a faulty item.

Refunding or replacing
The first two of these courses of action are usually straightforward

procedures which are clearly defined in the company systems. When a sale is made in the first instance, a transaction takes place to take an item out of stock and to take money into the system. This not only records the financial state of the business but also identifies stock which may need replacing for future sales. When a refund of money takes place, this also has to be recorded as a transaction to reverse the process and bring the item, albeit faulty, back into the system. An efficient organisation will be operating a method of stock control in order to ensure correct stock levels of the most popular items.

If an alternative item is offered in exchange for the faulty item, then again another transaction must be recorded for the new item to be taken out of stock.

The method of recording these transactions will depend on the systems operating within your company. Some may need handwritten documentation but on the more sophisticated EPOS electronic tills, this can be done by machine.

Alternative forms of compensation

For the other types of compensation, it may be discretionary and negotiable with the customer. If you have been able to ask the right questions and are able to judge what you think the customer may be happy with, you can offer a suggested settlement which you think will be acceptable to them. If you are allowed to make these decisions, then you will always offer the outcome that will be acceptable to the customer. Don't insult them by offering too little. But remember that the solution should be cost-effective to your company. Don't offer a 30 per cent discount when the problem is small and the customer would have been happy to accept 10 per cent.

Again, you must be sure of company policies regarding discretionary compensation. It may be that senior management are the only people who can make these decisions.

Finally, you also need to know what to do with the merchandise that has been returned. To leave it lying around the till area would be untidy and inefficient.

If the item is in perfect condition and can be offered for resale, you will need to understand the system for reticketing and re-entering the item into the stock records.

If the item is faulty, you need to understand the method of returning the item to the manufacturer or the company warehouse, whichever is appropriate. Each company has their own procedures for dealing with these activities. Ensure you fully understand how to deal with them. If something is not clear, ask your manager, your supervisor or an experienced colleague how.

ENCOURAGING COMPLAINTS

Do you believe that people who complain are a nuisance, and should be shut up and sent away?

Wrong. Complaints are an excellent opportunity. A customer who complains gives you the chance to:

- find out why they are unhappy
- prevent the same thing happening again
- put things right
- create customer loyalty.

If only all unhappy customers complained, retailers would be able to provide better service and quality. But many customers are too shy to ask to speak to the manager, or too busy to write a letter.

Experts estimate that only one in five dissatisfied customers complains. But the ones who don't have the time or courage to complain to the shop don't remain silent. Instead, each of them will tell, on average, seven people about the poor service they have received!

It is easy to understand how quickly a shop's reputation can be damaged by a handful of unhappy customers. Be grateful to those who tell *you*, instead of their neighbours, what annoys them.

Keeping your customers happy

Some shops hand out forms to their customers, inviting their comments, praise or complaints.

Encouraging customers to buy is important. But it is equally important to make them feel happy after they have made the purchase. If your customers are dissatisfied with what they have bought from your shop, and if they cannot exchange it for something else, they will probably not return.

If you don't respond correctly when somebody complains, you will lose also their custom.

HOW TO RESPOND

If a customer approaches you with a complaint, you should do the following:

1. Listen carefully.

2. Find out the reason for the complaint.

3. Write down the reason (perhaps on a complaint form).

4. Thank the customer for pointing out the matter.

5. Show the customer that you take them and the complaint seriously.

6. Apologise for the fault and the inconvenience, for example 'I'm sorry you've had this problem.' Even if you don't think the complaint is justified, you can say something non-committal such as 'I'm sorry to hear you are not happy about this.'

7. Say what you will do to put matters right.

8. Do it.

9. Follow your shop's procedure for documentation.

10. Make sure the customer is satisfied with the outcome.

Rejecting complaints

Even if a complaint is not justified, you should remain polite, listen carefully, and thank the customer for pointing out the problem. Apologise for not being able to help. If in doubt, ask a senior member of staff to take the decision. Sometimes it is better to accept a complaint even if the matter is not the shop's fault.

A complaining customer should leave the shop satisfied, whether their complaint was accepted or not.

CASE STUDIES

A refund without proof of purchase

Rebecca is working on the till when a customer comes towards her with a Streetwise bag in her hand.

'Can I have a refund on this please? My husband bought it for my birthday and the colour looks absolutely awful on me.'

'Do you have a receipt?' Rebecca asks.

'No, I'm sorry. My husband didn't give it to me and, to be honest, I'm going to change it for something else and I don't think he will even realise. That way I won't hurt his feelings,' she smiles.

Rebecca realises that the blouse is one of theirs, as it has a Streetwise label in. 'If you would like to go and try on a different colour, I will deal with it for you. Just leave this one here for now.'

Offering high standards of produce

Linda is busy on the till when a customer comes towards her with a pineapple in her hand.

'I got this home yesterday and when I cut it open it was all soft inside,' she says in a belligerent tone.

'I'm very sorry,' replies Linda. 'Would you like to just go and choose another one?'

The customer stands and looks at Linda in surprise. This obviously isn't what she had expected. The customer had been sure the assistant would accuse her of buying the pineapple a week ago and bruising it herself on the way home.

'Is that OK?' the customer asks, hesitating.

'Of course,' Linda replies. 'We don't like to think that our produce is not perfect. You will realise that it is impossible to see inside the pineapple. There are times when something like this slips through our quality control.'

The customer is pleased and quickly forgets what a disappointment the pineapple, which she had bought as a special treat, had been to her family.

Rebecca observes how not to do it

A woman comes into the Streetwise shop, and asks quietly to speak to the manager. Miss Turner, the owner and manager, is not in the shop today. The customer waits patiently until Mrs Baldock, the assistant manager, is available.

'I'm sorry to bother you, Mrs Baldock. I'm afraid this blouse I bought last week isn't very well made. You see, two of the seams came undone in the first wash. I mean, I could repair it, but then I've bought it new, and I thought Streetwise sold only good quality clothes, and this should not happen.'

Mrs Baldock, who is very busy this morning, doesn't believe the customer, and wants to get rid of her and return to her urgent work: 'All our garments are well made. You've probably washed it on the wrong cycle.'

The customer shakes her head: 'No, I washed it exactly as in the instructions, see here, it says "40 degrees, wash as synthetics".'

Mrs Baldock gets impatient. 'Anybody could say that. How can I know if you are telling the truth? Anyway, even if the seams have come undone, it's the manufacturer's fault, not ours.'

'But I want this blouse exchanged. This is the most expensive blouse I've ever bought. And I paid £3.60 just for the bus fare to get here to show you what it looks like.'

Finally, Mrs Baldock agrees to exchange the blouse for another one. But the customer doesn't want this type of blouse anymore. She fears that all blouses of this type are poorly made. She wants cash, so that she can buy another blouse, elsewhere. However, all Mrs Baldock offers is a voucher which the customer can use in the shop.

Rebecca, who has observed the scene, wonders if this customer will come again. 'Couldn't we have given her a cash refund?' she asks Mrs Baldock. But Mrs Baldock only says: 'If we start that, then everyone will want cash.'

Was the customer honest?

John is busy on the till in Off The Record when the next customer to be served is giving the impression of being very impatient. As the customer John is dealing with leaves, he looks up to smile at the next in line, but is met by a curt demand. 'I want my money back on this rubbish.'

'I'm sorry,' said John. 'Can you tell me what the problem is?'

'Look, this is no good. Obviously faulty manufacture. I want my money back.' This is in a loud voice and with a very aggressive manner.

John is doubtful that the disc was faulty. Perhaps the customer has changed his mind about the music he wanted. But why is he so aggressive? Did he perhaps damage it himself and is now being aggressive to cover up?

POINTS FOR DISCUSSION

1. Looking at the situation of the customer wanting to exchange her birthday present: Was Streetwise legally obliged to change the garment? Did the customer need a receipt? How did Rebecca know the garment had been bought at her branch? Was this important?

2. Have you ever returned a present to a store because it was not suitable? If yes, how were you treated by the sales assistant? How did you feel about it?

3. What would be the outcome of the confrontation between John and the angry customer if John became very firm and said the customer could not have a refund?

4. What would be the impact on other people in the shop if the discussion about getting a refund became very heated?

5. What would be the outcome if John politely and courteously gave the customer a refund? Which advantages and disadvantages would this course of action have?

6. Are there any other options open to John? Which course of action would you take in John's place?

7. Did Linda do the right thing by not asking the customer when she had bought the pineapple? In what other way might the situation have developed?

8. Can you remember a situation when you went to a shop to return an item, or to complain. How were you treated? How did you feel about it? If you were not happy with the outcome, how would you have liked to be treated by the sales assistant?

9. Rebecca still wonders if Mrs Baldock can be wrong. What do you think? Imagine that you are the assistant manager. How would you have responded? Which mistakes did Mrs Baldock make?

10. What if Mrs Baldock often alienates good customers with her behaviour? Should you inform Miss Turner, who has a high opinion of her experienced assistant manager's work? If no, give your reasons. If yes, explain how and when you would do this. Write down your answers.

6
Maintaining Health and Safety

You must know how to prevent accidents and danger at your workplace, and how to respond in an emergency to protect your customers, your colleagues and yourself.

LOOKING AT THE HEALTH AND SAFETY POLICY

Every shop should have a health and safety policy. This document should include:

1. An outline of the health and safety policy.

2. Instructions on how to carry out this policy.

3. The employer's and the employees' responsibilities in law.

4. Health and safety training (for example, first aid courses, or instructions on how to use machinery safely).

5. When and how the policy is to be updated and reviewed.

6. Instructions on how to report an accident.

7. Name(s) of the company's health and safety representative(s), and where to reach them.

8. Reference to disciplinary rules.

9. Codes of practice and references to literature.

10. How and where the policy should be displayed.

Getting to know your shop's policy

Do you know where it is kept in your shop? If your boss keeps it hidden in his or her drawer, ask if you can take a photocopy and display it on a noticeboard.

In some shops the policy is phrased in such a bureaucratic language that nobody understands it without reading it a dozen times. Write a summary in plain English, get it approved by your health and safety officer, and display it.

WHEN AN ACCIDENT OCCURS

If an accident happens, do the following:

1. Protect yourself. Don't approach without checking that it is safe. If your colleague has been knocked unconscious by a beam falling from the ceiling, you don't want to be injured by a second beam crashing down.

2. Give first aid to the injured person. If you cannot give first aid, call a colleague who is a trained first-aider.

3. Call an ambulance if someone has a serious injury.

4. Inform the shop or department manager, or the health and safety representative.

5. Ask the victim what has happened (if they are able to tell you), write the answer down.

6. Ask witnesses about their observations, and take notes.

7. Add your own observations, for example 'Floor was still slippery after cleaning' or 'Monica had felt faint all morning' or 'We noticed a smell of gas at about 10 am for the first time, but it disappeared soon.'

8. Record the details of any injury in the accident book (see below).

9. Take measures to prevent similar accidents in the future.

GIVING FIRST AID

Every shop must have a first aid cupboard or box for the staff. This should also be available if a customer needs help.

A first aid box kept 'somewhere in the office, probably in one of the drawers' is of little use in an emergency. The equipment must be easy to find for everyone. All colleagues should know where it is, and outsiders should be able to find it in an emergency, too.

You may want to display a note at the counter, in the toilets and other strategic places saying, for example: 'First aid box in the bottom shelf at cashpoint one.' The first aid box must be marked with a white cross on a green background.

People have the habit of taking what they need from the first aid box and relying on 'someone' to replace the items.

Adhesive plasters disappear quickly. People use them whenever they have a little cut on their finger or have grazed their knee. It is right to use plaster to prevent dirt getting into a wound, however small, and to stop the blood from staining the merchandise. However, you may find that in an emergency there is no plaster left. Safety pins tend to disappear quickly too – they are so useful when a button has come off or a hem has come down.

Check regularly – say, every three months – if the supplies are still complete; restock as necessary.

Becoming a first-aider

Employers who have more than a certain number of staff must also see to it that there are trained first-aiders. If there aren't any first-aiders among the staff, the employer must arrange for one or more employees to go on a training course.

Whether your store needs first-aiders, and how many, depends not only on the number of staff, but also on the type of merchandise sold, and specific hazards. Details can be found in *Code of Practice COP 42* (ISBN 0118855360). This book costs £3 and is available from St John Supplies, Tel. 0171 278 7888.

You may want to volunteer to train as a first-aider. Your employer will probably give you the time off – four days – and pay for the course. The skills you learn will be a bonus at any workplace, and the qualification will enhance your CV.

St John's and the Red Cross organise First Aid At The Workplace courses; you can find their addresses in your local telephone directory.

A good first-aid manual is usually included in the cost of a first-aid

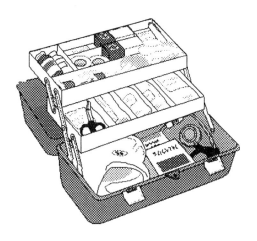

Your first aid kit must contain

An easy-to-follow instruction card

A box of adhesive plasters in various sizes

20 sterile dressings

6 triangular bandages

6 safety pins

A pair of scissors

6 medium, 2 large and 3 extra large wound dressings

2 sterile eyepads with attachments

Depending on how many people are employed at your workplace, on the type of work they do and the machinery they use, extra equipment may be necessary.

Fig. 11. Contents of a first aid kit.

First aid:
Treating unconscious victims

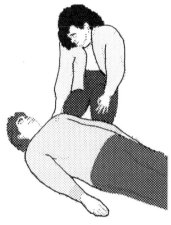

1. If you discover someone lying on the floor, make sure there is no immediate danger to yourself. Then talk to the victim. Ask what has happened. Touch them. See if they respond.

2. If they don't talk or move, check if they are breathing. Place your ear above their mouth, look along chest and tummy area to hear, feel and see if there is any breathing.

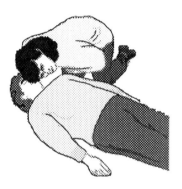

3. If the person is breathing and does not seem to have any injuries, place them in the recovery position. If you don't know how to do this, just turn them gently to lie on their side. Ask a colleague to help you with this, if possible. Support them with boxes or bags on either side.

Fig. 12. Treating unconscious victims.

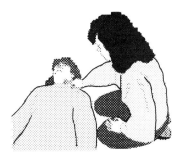

4. If a victim does not breathe, check if their heart is still beating. Place your fingertips on their neck and feel for the pulse. If you cannot feel the pulse, call the ambulance immediately. Saving a life can be a matter of seconds now.

5. If you can feel the pulse, but the victim is not breathing, tilt their head backwards. You can do this by lifting the chin and pressing the forehead backwards. If you can, open their mouth and check if their is any loose matter (for example, dentures or food) obstructing the airway, and remove it.

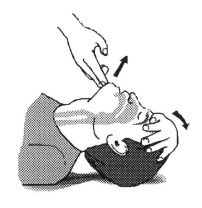

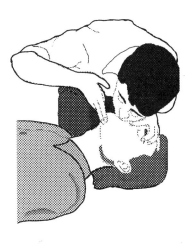

If the victim still does not breathe, give mouth-to-mouth ventilation. If there is no trained first aider, do it yourself. Start at once. Inhale deeply, then breathe slowly into the victim's mouth, at the speed you normally breathe. Pinch their nostrils together. For children, use a smaller amount of air. If another person is available, ask them to call an ambulance while you are giving mouth-to-mouth ventilation.

course. However, if you or your store want to buy a book, consider *First Aid Manual* (ISBN 086 3189 78 4), £8.99, also available from St John Supplies.

Treating unconscious victims

If you discover someone lying on the floor, make sure there is no immediate danger to yourself. Then talk to the victim – ask what has happened. Touch them. See if they respond.

If they don't talk or move, check if they are breathing. Place your ear above their mouth, look along chest and tummy area to hear, feel and see if there is any breathing.

If they don't breathe, tilt their head backwards by lifting the chin and pressing the forehead backwards. If you can, open their mouth and check if there is any loose matter (dentures, food) obstructing the airway, and remove it.

If they still don't breathe, check their pulse. Do this with your fingertips on their neck. If there is no pulse, it probably means that the heart has stopped beating. Call the ambulance immediately. Every second counts now to save a life.

If the heart beats, but they don't breathe, give mouth-to-mouth ventilation. If there is no trained first-aider, you can do it by inhaling deeply, then breathing slowly into the victim's mouth, at the speed you normally breathe. For children, use a smaller amount of air.

If they breathe, but are unconscious, place them in the recovery position (lying on their side).

Treating shock victims

If someone is conscious and without any visible injury, they may still be suffering from shock. Symptoms include shivering, cold sweat, and talking nonsense.

Get them to lie down. Raise their legs as high as possible, using boxes, suitcases or whatever comes to hand. Cover them with a blanket. Talk to them in a calm, reassuring manner.

Other injuries

If you suspect a fracture (broken bone), don't attempt to splint it. Ask the person not to move the limb and not to put any weight on it, and take them to the nearest hospital for an X-ray and, if appropriate, a plaster. A person with a suspected head injury should also be taken to the hospital.

If you believe someone has internal injuries, don't move them (unless you have to get them out of immediate danger, *eg* a burning building). Call an ambulance.

KEEPING THE ACCIDENT BOOK

Every accident must be entered in the accident book. Some accident victims insist that it is not necessary. They don't want to be regarded as 'weaklings'. Ignore their protests. Enter every accident, however minor. Even if your colleague who slipped and fell in the car park only grazed her knee, a complication may occur later. What looks like a harmless scratch now may get infected and develop into a nasty wound.

Record the following:

- The date and time when the incident happened.

- The name, occupation, age of the victim.

- The type of injury and where exactly it is (not 'bleeding knee' but 'bleeding left knee').

- The exact place the accident happened (*eg* 'just outside the back entrance').

- A brief description of what happened, and how.

- The name of the person who gave first aid.

If a serious accident (one which causes death or major injury) or dangerous occurrence (a 'near miss') happens, the Health and Safety Executive must be told.

FIGHTING A FIRE

Do you know where the fire extinguishers are kept? Do you and your colleagues know how to use them? If not, ask for a demonstration and practice. In an emergency, you won't have time to read a firefighting instruction book.

Your shop should have the fire procedure written down and displayed where everyone can see it. Fire exits should be marked clearly. Never block a fire exit, not even when you think you need extra storage space for a few hours.

If you discover a fire and it is small, extinguish it by throwing something over it, for example, a coat or a blanket, or use the fire extinguisher. If you don't succeed immediately, raise the alarm.

Don't keep trying to extinguish a fire if this would put you at risk.

Stay calm. Call the fire service, and inform your colleagues. Reassure the customers and get them out of the shop safely. Look after frail people and children in particular. Close all windows and doors in the building if you can do it without risk.

Don't go back to get personal belongings, goods or equipment from a room where there is a fire or smoke. Don't allow customers or colleagues to go back either. Meet at the agreed assembly place and check that everyone is there.

Preventing fire

Tidiness is the best precaution, because rubbish and litter which is left lying in a corner can easily start to burn if it is exposed to heat or an open flame.

Store any flammable or volatile liquids carefully. The smallest quantity of some liquids can be a fire hazard.

RAISING THE ALARM

When you dial 999 because of an accident, fire or other emergency, make sure you pass the following information on:

1. Who is calling? State your name and the name of the shop. This is essential in case your emergency call gets cut off.

2. What has happened?

3. The address of the shop.

4. How many people are injured?

5. What type of injuries? You don't have to give a precise diagnosis, but something along the lines of 'bleeds heavily from the thigh' or 'large burns on the back and the legs' is useful.

RECOGNISING SAFETY HAZARDS

On the sales floor

Frequent safety hazards include: spills, broken bottles, fruit peels, cabbage leaves on the floor, uneven floors, trailing wires, cartons left in gangways, badly stacked goods, racks and counters with sharp edges and corners, insecure shelves, ill-maintained trolleys which are difficult to steer, fixtures with loose screws and bits of metal sticking out, and splintering wood.

In the office
Accidents are likely to be caused by tea kettles, electrical shorts, trailing wires, and collapsing furniture.

In the storeroom
Accidents occur because of goods falling from high, because staff lift goods which are too heavy, wrongly or carelessly used fork lifts or carton balers, and heavy and awkward doors.

Lifting and carrying
A frequent cause for accidents in shops is lifting and carrying. If you lift something, get close to the item. If it is bulky, crouch down with your legs bent. Keep the back upright, and don't bend over the item. Grip the load firmly so it won't slip. Use your legs to lift the load, keep the back straight. Hold the load close to you.

Carry the item so that your hands don't get knocked against shelves. Don't get your fingers trapped when you set down or stack your load.

If your job involves a lot of heavy carrying, wear sturdy shoes. If you work in the storeroom and the boxes are very heavy, your toes are vulnerable. Consider shoes which are reinforced with steel toecaps.

If an item is too heavy for you to lift alone, ask a colleague to help. You don't have to show what a strong man you are. If your employer provides lifting equipment, use it, but first find out how.

DEALING WITH BREAKAGES AND SPILLAGES

If there is a breakage or spillage, clear it up at once. If you cannot do it immediately, use a warning sign or something similar to draw the customers' attention to it. You can also place an upturned chair or a wire basket over it. Have sand or special absorbing material at hand.

If an irritating or poisonous substance has been spilled, alert your manager. There may be strict rules for the cleaning-up procedure. Do you know which substances at your work-place have been assessed under the Control of Substances Hazardous to Health (COSHH) Regulations? If not, ask your health and safety representative or your manager.

Don't let customers use the floor until it is clean and dry again.

DISPOSING OF WASTE AND RUBBISH

Waste and rubbish quickly become a safety hazard if they are not disposed of regularly. But the disposal itself can be dangerous if you don't do it properly and carefully.

CASE STUDIES

Rebecca fills in the accident book

'Do you have a plaster?' asks Alan, a work-experience student at Streetwise. 'I've just cut my hand. It doesn't hurt, I just don't want to bleed all over the clothes.'

'How did it happen?' asks Rebecca while she gets a large plaster out. She observes that the thumb is bleeding strongly.

He shrugs. 'Oh, it's nothing. Just a piece of sharp metal sticking out from the shelf near the door. Stupid of me, really, I should have taken more care.'

'We'd better enter it in the accident book,' she decides. But Alan protests: 'Look, it's almost stopped bleeding. It's not an accident. It doesn't even hurt. I don't want any fuss about it.'

Rebecca laughs. 'You're probably right and it's nothing. But just in case the cut gets infected or there are any problems later on, you'll want proof that it happened here at work. Anyway, it's good practice for me to learn how to fill in the accident book. I don't often get the chance to use it in this shop.'

After reporting the details of the 'accident' in the book, she says: 'And now let's have a look at that piece of metal and what we can do about it. We don't want it to cause any serious injuries to anybody.'

John discovers several hazards in the shop

Over the last couple of weeks, several accidents have occurred at Off The Record.

John unpacked and sorted new leaflets, and cut his hand between the thumb and index finger. The bleeding stopped soon, and he forgot about the little injury. But in the afternoon, when he was arranging a display of LPs, a record cover got stuck between his fingers, tore the wound open. This time the wound bled much stronger; blood dripped on the records and the carpet. Three days later, the injury still hasn't healed fully.

A ten-year-old boy, whose mother was browsing, ran against a display case and hurt the back of his head. He was bleeding heavily, and screaming. The only trained first-aider in the shop works part-time, and it was her day off.

Nobody among the staff knew if there was a first aid kit and where to find it. John borrowed one from a neighbouring shop, but nobody knew how to apply a bandage to the head. Alerted by the screams, several passers-by came into the shop to see what was going on. John wondered if he should call an ambulance; and if yes, if 999 was the right number to dial.

On another occasion an elderly woman who could not find the record she was after, looked at a pile of cardboard boxes stacked in a corner of the shop. She opened the top one. It did not contain records, but metal units for a shelving system. When she pushed the box back, it lost balance and fell on her left foot. She screamed with pain, hobbled a few steps, and fell.

This time, John knew where to find the first aid kit, but he did not know how to treat a probably broken foot. The old woman began to tremble and shiver. Her face was pale and damp with sweat. John asked her name, but she only repeated the sentence 'tomorrow I'll have fish and chips'.

Another customer slipped on the freshly cleaned and still damp stairs. Luckily, she only had a couple of bruises and a grazed knee.

An accident book exists for staff accidents; but nobody bothers to enter anything. In the case of customer accidents, no records are kept.

Linda reacts promptly

It's a busy Saturday morning. Linda is restocking shelves in the groceries section at Westmores. One customer bumps into another who drops two bottles of coke. The bottles break; there are many pieces of glass, and the coke spills over the floor.

Linda's first instinct is to rush for a piece of cloth, a brush and a dustpan. However, she fears that someone might slip on the wet sticky floor and fall into the pieces of glass while she is away.

She places several cases around the area of spillage. No colleague is in sight at this moment, so she asks a friendly customer to keep an eye on the spillage for a minute while she dashes to get a bucket of water, a cloth, a brush and a dustpan. Luckily, these are kept in an easily accessible place.

She also gets a stand-up sign, 'Caution – wet floor' which she places on the floor after she has wiped it thoroughly.

POINTS FOR DISCUSSION

1   Looking at the shop where you are employed, answer the following:

   (a) Which types of rubbish and waste occur regularly?

   (b) How and where are they stored?

   (c) Which of them can be safety hazards?

   (d) Is there any protective clothing or equipment for handling certain types of waste? If yes, describe the clothing or equipment and its use.

   (e) How often, by whom and how is the waste being removed?

   (f) Which of your colleagues are trained in first aid?

   (g) Who is your health and safety officer?

   (h) Where is the accident book kept?

   (i) Where is the first aid box kept?

   (j) How many fire extinguishers are in the building, and where?

   (k) Do you know where the health and safety policy is displayed in the shop?

   (l) Do you understand it fully? Do your colleagues understand it?

2.   Imagine you are John Anderson at Off The Record. What would you have done when the elderly woman injured her foot?

3.   Mr Gregory, manager of Off The Record, wants to make the shop safer for both customers and employees. He asks John to develop a new policy on how to deal with accidents in the shop, and how to prevent them. All the measures must be suitable to be carried out within a month.

      Imagine you are John. Look at the causes of recent accidents.

Make several suggestions as to how similar incidents can be prevented in the future. Then look at the way the staff responded to the incidents. Develop a policy on how to deal with accidents. Add any suggestion your manager should consider.

7
Preventing Theft

Have you always wanted to be a detective? When you are working in a shop, you have the opportunity. You need an alert eye, the gift of observation, quick thinking, and diplomacy.

As a detective, you want to catch the thieves red-handed. But more importantly, you want to make it impossible for them to steal anything. This is a difficult task, especially when you are busy and the shop is crowded. But you can achieve a lot if you understand how thieves operate. If you know their tricks, you can foil them. This chapter provides you with a crash course in crime detection and prevention.

HOW TO BE A DETECTIVE

You can learn from professional store detectives. They:

- know all the shoplifter's tricks
- have an alert mind
- keep their eyes open all the time, even when they are busy
- know how to challenge a suspected thief without drawing other people's attention
- act quickly but remain calm
- don't let a suspect provoke them
- stay polite at all times
- prevent theft happening in the first place.

SEEING THROUGH SHOPLIFTERS' TRICKS

Shoplifters won't fool you if you know their tricks.

Trick 1

Most shoplifters seek out shops which have a complicated layout, narrow aisles and high shelves, where the staff cannot keep an eye on every area. Many exits, especially exits far away from the tills, encourage shoplifters who think they can get away quickly. Thieves are particularly active when they notice that a shop is crowded or understaffed, for example during lunch hours and on Saturday mornings.

Trick 2

The shoplifters bring used carrier bags into the shop, usually the shop's own bags. They put the stolen goods into the bag and behave as if they had bought the goods.

Trick 3

Two shoplifters work as a pair. One distracts the sales assistant by asking for a complicated demonstration. The second shoplifter uses the time to steal.

Trick 4

The shoplifter compares several items, then quickly switches the prices, takes the more expensive item to the checkout, and pays the lower price.

Trick 5

Thieves work in gangs. One of them knocks over a big shelf-full of liquid or fragile goods, or does something else which attracts the attention of all the staff and customers for a while. The other thieves quickly fill their bags and leave the shop.

Trick 6

This is a variation of trick 5. Shoplifter 1 brings a big shopping bag. Shoplifter 2, usually an older person, starts shrieking or feigning a heart attack several aisles away, attracting the attention of the staff, while shoplifter 1 fills her bag and disappears.

Trick 7

Yet another variation. Shoplifter 1 reports to the staff that there is a shoplifter in a particular aisle (which is, of course, at the opposite end of the shop to where shoplifter 2 is filling a bag). To avoid being suspected themselves, shoplifter 1 stays in the shop a while longer, so that nobody can connect them with the person with the big bag.

Trick 8
The thief pretends to consider an item, takes it out of the shop to see it in daylight, and doesn't return.

Trick 9
The thief takes two items into the fitting room on one hanger, so it looks like only one. Out of sight in the fitting room, one item goes into the shopping bag. The thief calmly comes out and returns the other item.

Trick 10
Shoplifters walk up and down the aisles, placing items in their bags without pausing, whenever the security camera is behind them rather than in front of them.

Trick 11
Shoplifter 1 is the person who takes the item from the shelf. Shoplifter 2 stands in a different part of the shop, apparently studying the items on display, with a large open bag placed on the floor. Shoplifter 1 walks around the shop and casually drops the item into shoplifter 2's bag. Unless there is a witness for the transaction, nobody can prove that shoplifter 1 has stolen anything (they don't have the stolen goods on them), and nobody suspects shoplifter 2 who wasn't even in the area where the theft occurred.

Trick 12
The shoplifter behaves suspiciously and makes sure someone observes him take an expensive item, for example a small portable TV, and hides it in his pocket or under his jacket. He goes straight to the exit. But just before he leaves the shop, he discards the 'stolen' item in a bin or on a cluttered shelf.

He wants to be seen taking the item, but he does not want to be observed getting rid of it. What he really wants is the management accusing him of theft, if possible with many witnesses. Sometimes he even has a mate who just 'happens' to be in the shop, shouting: 'Look they've caught a shoplifter', to attract crowds. Or the mate may say: 'I would never have thought that of you, Joe. Just wait until your boss hears of this. And what is your girlfriend going to say?'

Of course, the body search proves that the shoplifter has no stolen goods on him. Now the 'innocent' makes a lot of fuss, claiming that his reputation was damaged because he was accused of theft in front of many people. He demands a financial compensation for all the suffering and embarrassment.

DISCOURAGING THIEVES

There are several ways in which your shop can discourage thieves:

1. Keep the layout of the shop clear and simple, and the shelves in the middle of the room fairly low. If necessary, use mirrors which allow the staff to look into all parts of the shop.

2. Keep small and valuable items in a place where staff can see them all the time, *eg* at the checkout.

3. If the shop can afford it, employ uniformed security staff or a plain-clothes shop detective.

4. Use hidden or visible closed-circuit TV video cameras.

5. Put up warning signs ('Security system in operation', 'Shoplifters' will be prosecuted').

6. Keep all parts of the shop well lit.

7. Allow customers to view an item outside the shop only if you or a colleague can escort them.

8. Watch people who carry crumpled carrier bags (most of them re-use bags because they care about the environment, but some may use the bags for shoplifting).

9. If one customer needs your full attention, ask a colleague to keep a watchful eye on the area.

DEALING WITH SUSPECTS

Don't accuse anyone of stealing unless you are able to prove it. If you shout 'Stop! Thief! I've seen you stealing a diamond ring!' and the accused turns out to be innocent, you have lost a customer. The person may even accuse you of defamation of character.

A polite method is to go to the person, and say: 'Excuse me, madam/ sir. I think you may have taken a CD from the shop and forgotten to pay for it.'

If the person is a thief, he or she will probably hand over the stolen goods without arguing. Leave it at that; you have succeeded.

Maybe the customer has really forgotten to pay for the CD. This can happen. They will be grateful, but embarrassed. They will be glad if you don't draw other people's attention to their error.

If the person is innocent – perhaps they don't have a CD on them, or they have already paid for it, or bought it from another shop – they will be annoyed. Apologise for the misunderstanding. If you were discreet and polite, they will appreciate that you were doing your duty.

Confronting a suspected thief, step-by-step

When confronting a suspected shoplifter, be polite. It may sound strange, but you should avoid accusing, threatening, obstructing or touching them. The best detectives use their brains instead of force.

1. Ask the suspect to come back into the store. Take him or her to a private place, out of the sight of customers.

2. Get a colleague as a witness. If possible, ask a senior member of staff, ideally a man if the suspect is male, or a woman if the suspect is female.

3. Observe the person closely – suspects may try to dump the stolen goods and thus the evidence.

4. Some shoplifters claim they need to go to the toilet, where they flush the stolen items down, or they use it as an opportunity to escape. You can't deny them the right to go to the toilet – but you can go with them, or send a colleague of the same sex as the suspect as an escort.

5. Don't let the suspect make a phone call. Perhaps they really need to make a call, for example to tell a friend they can't meet them for lunch because they have been delayed. But it can be a trick. Simple phrases such as 'I have been delayed' or 'Feed the dog' or 'Dinner's in the freezer' can be coded messages which mean 'I have been caught.

Remove all stolen goods kept at home.'
Ask the suspect to wait until the police arrives.

6. Tell the suspected shoplifter what you have seen. Ask them to empty their pockets and bags. But don't do a body search. Leave that to the police.

7. If you are sure that it was theft, call the police.

8. If the suspected thief tries to escape, you have the right to detain them, but you should use only as much force as is absolutely necessary.

If a suspect refuses to come into the shop

Some suspects will provoke you to accuse them, for example, by shouting: 'What, you are calling me a thief?' Don't let them provoke you; don't accuse them of anything at this stage (remember trick 12!). But have a good look at them, and remember their features. If they escape, the police will appreciate a description.

If necessary, you can make a citizen's arrest. For this, you have to tell them what you are arresting them for. For example, 'I am arresting you for theft of a CD.' Again, use as little force as possible.

Warning: It can be impossible, or dangerous to make a citizen's arrest. In this case, just memorise the suspect's facial features, height, clothing *etc*, and call the police. Don't put yourself at risk.

CASE STUDIES

Rebecca escorts a customer

A young woman at Streetwise shows interest in several items from a range of silk clothes: a jacket, a blouse, a skirt and a pair of trousers.

'I've always wanted clothes which I could mix and match,' she explains to Rebecca. 'I almost bought a similar combination at another shop. But when I looked at them closely, it turned out that they were slightly different shades of blue! Are these all the same shade? It's difficult to judge in the artificial light.'

Rebecca smiles. 'You are right; sometimes even items from the same range have a slight variation because of the dying process. Let's go outside and have a look at it in daylight, to make sure.'

She escorts the customer, who finds that the colours match perfectly.

John suspects a thief

Working at Off The Record, John observes a teenager dropping a cassette into his bag. He leaves the shop without paying. John follows the boy outside and confronts him politely: 'Excuse me, I think you may have taken a cassette and forgotten to pay. Can you please come into the office to clarify this matter?'

The boy agrees to come into the office, and he shows the cassette in question. The cassette is clearly an old one: it has no clingfilm, and the tape has been pulled out and is damaged.

'I've borrowed my brother's tapes for a party without his permission,' explains the boy. 'I've damaged this one, and I want to replace it without my brother noticing. I took the old one into the shop to make sure I bought the same cassette. You had several cassettes by the same band, so I took mine out to compare, and when I saw there wasn't the right one, I put the old one back in the bag.'

John realises he has made a mistake. 'I'm very sorry; I see this was a misunderstanding. I do apologise.'

The boy takes it well: 'That's alright. You were just doing your job. It was stupid of me, really, I should have explained what I wanted instead of trying myself.'

John is glad that this customer is so understanding. He apologises again, and accompanies the customer to the door.

Linda copes with an emergency

It's a busy Saturday morning at Westmores, when a curious incident happens. It appears that a customer has run a shopping trolley forcefully into a gondola full of liqueur bottles, knocking it over. This would have taken a lot of force, and the customer is nowhere to be seen. However, several members of staff and many customers crowd around the scene to see what has happened.

Linda hurries to clean up the mess and secure the area to prevent an accident. While she gets the cleaning materials and the warning sign, she notices several people in the next aisle filling huge leather bags with expensive spirits.

Linda has no experience in dealing with such a situation. However, the assistant manager, Ms Harrison, has come out of the office because she heard the noise.

Linda takes her to the side and says quietly: 'I think there are shoplifters in the next aisle; two tall women and one man, all with big brown leather bags.'

Ms Harrison goes to confront the suspects who are just making for the exit, and Linda continues cleaning away the broken bottles without drawing any attention to what else is going on.

POINTS FOR DISCUSSION

In the case studies, everything went well. But sometimes, the situation can become tricky and call for your judgement and diplomacy. Let's imagine the same situations, but with added complications.

1. Imagine your are Rebecca. It's lunchtime, and you and Miss Turner are the only staff. There are several customers waiting to be served, and Miss Turner is engaged by one customer who demands particular attention. The lighting is admittedly poor. You cannot say if it's the same shade of blue either. The customer insists on taking the garments outside. She is not alone; her husband is with her, and he seems short tempered.

   How do you respond? You want to keep the customer happy, and you want to protect the goods. There are several possible ways of dealing with the situation. Explain why your chosen solution is best in terms of customer care and security.

2. Imagine the boy John suspected of shoplifting but who is innocent, is not understanding at all. 'You have accused me! All my mates have seen it, and they will spread the word. You have made me lose face in front of all the others! It's so embarrassing. All the people in the street who have seen me taken into the shop will think I'm a thief. You have effectively ruined my prospects of finding a job locally, and I've been trying so hard.' The boy gets more and more agitated and genuinely seems to believe that his reputation is ruined.

   How should John respond? Write down what John could say to calm the customer and to save the situation. Again, there are several possible approaches. Tip: Remember that as a trainee, and even as a qualified member of staff, you don't have to cope with tricky situations on your own.

3. In Linda's case, it was convenient that Ms Harrison was at hand. But what if the incident had happened at lunchtime, with no customers (other than the suspected shoplifters), and the only other member of

staff present was a fifteen-year-old work-experience student?

Think carefully, then write down how you would handle the situation in Linda's place. Don't forget the dangerous spillage.

8
Communicating at the Workplace

All activities in a shop depend on people communicating with each other: by talking to each other face-to-face, on the phone, or by writing.

By communicating, people pass on information. Poor communication can mean wrong information, or not enough information. This costs money, time and patience.

HANDLING PHONE CALLS

Telephone calls can come from another department, or from outside. Some modern telephone systems show a light flashing or use a different tone when the call is coming from outside. But if in doubt, treat every call as an outside call.

Taking incoming calls
When answering the telephone it is as important to make the right impression as it is when face-to-face with a customer.

1. Answer the telephone quickly, if possible between the second and the eighth ring. Don't keep callers waiting longer than that.

2. Start with 'Good morning' or 'Good afternoon'. The first two spoken words can be difficult to understand, so it is good to begin with a phrase which the caller can guess.

3. Identify the company, then yourself. 'Good morning. This is Off The Record, John Anderson speaking.' Or 'Good afternoon. This is Streetwise, Rebecca Smith speaking.'

4. If you know the call comes from within the store, you can give the name of the department where you are working: 'Good afternoon, sales department, Rebecca Smith speaking.'

5. Find out what the caller wants. You can say, 'Can I help you'. But this usually results in the comment: 'Well, I don't know if you can.' It's better to say 'How can I help you?' or 'How may I help you?'

6. If you can't help the caller put them through to someone who can. But tell the caller that you are transferring them. Otherwise they may think you have cut them off.
    'Just one moment, Mrs Nag, I'll put you through to the manager, Mr Knight.'

7. Don't put anyone through until you've found out who they are. If they haven't given you their name, ask politely: 'May I ask who's calling?'

8. If the caller asks for a specific person, say: 'Certainly. Just one moment, I'm putting you through.' If you are not certain that the phone call is welcome at that moment, say: 'I'll check if Mr Knight is free to take your call now. Would you like to hold the line, please?'

9. If you cannot connect the caller with the person they want to speak to, because the line is busy, say: 'I'm afraid the line is busy. Would you like to try again later?' or 'I'm afraid he's on the phone. Shall I ask him to ring you back?' or 'I'm afraid Mr Knight is on the phone. Would you like to speak to the assistant manager, Ms Harrison?'

0. Keep pen and paper at hand, in case the caller wishes to leave a message. Make sure you have all the details: the caller's full name, the name of the company, the phone number, who they want to speak to, the purpose of their call, the date and time they phoned, and your name or initials.

11. Don't be shy to ask them to repeat their name if you did not catch it when they first mentioned it. Ask them to spell it, if necessary.

12. Tell the caller what you are going to do. For example: 'I will pass your message on to our book-keeper, Ms Fugger.' – 'I'll ring you back tomorrow morning.' – 'I will ask Mr Knight to phone you.' – 'I will send you the brochure and price list as soon as they are available.' And make sure you do what you promised to do!

13. Try to smile when you speak. The person on the other end of the line can 'hear' your smile.

TELEPHONE NOTE

Message for: John Anderson

Date of call: 20 September 19XX

Time: 9·30 am

Note taken by: Brian Barrow

Caller: Sue Singer of Saul Ltd

Tel. no.:   ooOo/ooooo

Message: Has the information you want about folk
                    music CDs. Please phone today (before
                    2·30 pm) or tomorrow.

Fig. 13. An example of a telephone note.

Making a phone call

The following are some important points to remember when making a
telephone call.

1. Keep a list of the phone numbers you need most frequently near the
   telephone. These should include external and internal numbers. It also
   helps to have a copy of the local telephone directory and of the *Yellow
   Pages* near the phone. If there isn't the space, you should at least know
   where these directories are kept.

2. Choose a time which is convenient for the person you are calling, as
   well as for yourself. If lunchtime is a busy time in your shop, postpone
   your call until after lunch. If your suppliers are extremely busy during
   the early morning hours, phone them in the afternoon instead. Of course
   this is not always possible: some phone calls cannotor must not be
   delayed.

3. Write down what you want to say or ask. This saves both your time
   and the other person's time, and cuts down on phone bills.

4. When the other person answers the phone, begin with the greeting, then identify your company and yourself: 'Good morning, this is John Anderson of Off The Record.'

5. If you want to be transferred to a person or a department, still identify yourself. Then ask: 'May I speak to Mrs Nag please?' or 'Please put me through to your accounts department.'

6. When you are phoning a big company, and don't know which department or person to ask for, state your purpose as briefly as you can. 'I want to find out about stationery supplies for a retail business.'

KEEPING SECRETS

Always be helpful when dealing with phone calls or enquiries. However, there is one limit to your helpfulness. Don't reveal confidential information. It can be difficult to judge whether certain information is confidential, and whether you should tell the person who is asking, especially if they ask casually, or in an important manner, clearly expecting you to answer.

Whether you should give the information or not, depends on who is asking for it, and why. Enquiries can come from members of the press, from charities, from sales representatives, from pressure groups, from students on a research project, or from local councillors. Always be courteous and helpful, even if you decide not to give the requested information.

If in doubt, play for time. Say you will ring them back, think the matter over, and consult your manager.

What not to tell
Information you should not disclose to outsiders without checking with your manager are the names, addresses and phone numbers of customers and colleagues, any security procedures, financial information, and your personal critical opinion.

RECEIVING AND RELAYING ORAL MESSAGES

You relay and receive many oral messages every day.

Examples

'Mrs Alfred phoned to say that she does not want to order the Beethoven symphonies. She has found another shop where they had them in stock.'

'Carol, I've just noticed that we have run out of fabric softener. Will you tell Ms Harrison please?'

'I'm off now. If Mr Peck comes while I'm on holiday, will you just give him the blue bag on my desk? It contains the book he forgot in the shop last week.'

Receiving a message

When you get a message:

- Acknowledge it.

- Repeat the message aloud, to make sure that you have understood it correctly and to help you memorise it.

- Write it down. Even if you think you will remember the message, you may forget to take action if many other things happen, or you may forget some of the details.

- Say what you are going to do about it. In the above examples, your response could be: 'All right, I will destroy the order note.' – 'Certainly. I will tell her when she returns after lunch.' – 'The blue bag on your desk? Yes, I will give it to Mr Peck when he comes to collect it.'

Relaying a message

When you relay a message:

- Say clearly what you have to say.

- Also say what you want the other person to do about it. Misunderstandings happen when the other person thinks you are taking action, while you meant them to handle the case.

- Make sure they have understood the message. Ask, for example: 'Have you got the details?', 'Will you be able to do this?', or 'Do you need any further information?'

- Repeat the message if necessary.

- Always be courteous and polite. Don't get impatient if someone doesn't understand what you want.

WRITTEN MESSAGES

A memo (memorandum) is an internal message. Many companies have pre-printed memo forms. These can be filled in quickly by hand or with a typewriter.

A typical memo form contains the following headings:

From: _____

To: _____

Date: _____

Re: _____

Message: _____

The advantages of memos are that they are not forgotten as easily as oral messages, and the person who wrote the memo has proof that he or she has done it. Memos are useful to give advance warning of events, for example a staff training session, and everyone gets a copy.

Another occasion when a written message is important is when a manager warns an employee – eg, the second warning that she must not smoke in the shop.

On the other hand, memos can be remote and impersonal, and they are often unsuitable for urgent matters.

In some companies staff spend a lot of time writing memos to each other, writing acknowledgements that they have received the memo, and even memos reminding their colleagues of the previous memo. Several copies are made of each memo, filed in many different folders. It takes a lot of composing, typing, reading and filing time. It wastes time and paper. This is called a 'memo culture'. You don't want a 'memo culture' developing in your store.

It is always useful, however, to have a record that the memo has been read – ask the recipients to return it with their initials, and keep a log of memos.

MEMO

From: Andrew Knight

To: Louise Harrison
               Kevin Ray
               Linda Cooke
               Susan Brown
               Mike Smith

Date: 12 March 19XX

Re: Security

Message: Can you please attend a staff meeting on Monday
               18 March 19XX, 9 am, in the staff canteen, for a
               briefing and discussion about store security?

               You will hear about the proposed new security
               cameras. I would also welcome your suggestions
               how to improve security in the areas in which you
               are working. The meeting will last about one hour. I
               have already informed your supervisors/managers
               that you will attend this meeting. If you are unable
               to attend, please let me know (ext. 37).

Fig. 14. An example of a memo.

RECEIVING AND DIRECTING VISITORS

Visitors to a shop include:

- suppliers
- sales representatives
- merchandisers
- demonstrators
- journalists
- maintenance staff
- health and safety inspectors
- trading standards inspectors
- groups – *eg* students or pupils – on a project
- applicants for a job
- police.

Checking visitors' identification
If someone comes to the shop and you don't know them, you should take some or all of the following steps, depending on your shop's policy:

- Ask their name, and the purpose of their visit.

- Ask them to sign the visitors' book.

- Ask for identification. Maintenance people, for example, will usually carry an identification card. A journalist will have a press card, and an inspector on an unannounced visit will show their identification automatically.

- Give each visitor a numbered badge, and enter the number in the visitors' book (this is done in large stores only).

Checklist
Are they who they claim to be?

1. Look closely at the authority document or ID card: is it valid? Does it look 'real' on close inspection?

2. If in doubt, phone the company or organisation they claim to represent. But don't phone the number they give you; it could be phoney too. Look up the correct number in the phone book.

3. Is the person they have come to see expecting them? If not, is he or she available?

4. If the person they have come to see cannot receive them immediately, don't leave the visitors unsupervised. Offer them a seat in the reception, or in an office where a colleague is working. Don't let them wander through the building.

Remember, however, to make the visitors feel welcome. Security is important, but don't let them feel that you suspect them.

Example
Visitor: 'Good morning. My name is Hotch, Mrs Louisa Hotch. I've come to see Ms Harrison, please.'

Sales assistant: 'Is Ms Harrison expecting you?'

Visitor: 'No, I don't think she is. I haven't had the time to phone. But it is important.'

Sales assistant: 'Certainly, Mrs Hotch. I'll see if Ms Harrison is free to see you now. May I tell her the purpose of your visit?'

Visitor: 'It's about the special event at the town hall on Saturday. She has booked space for a stall to promote the shop, and now it seems that all the available spaces have been double-booked by error.'

Sales assistant: 'Just a moment, Mrs Hotch.'

(phones): 'Ms Harrison? I've got a Mrs Hotch here to see you. She wants to discuss our stall at the town hall event; it appears there is a problem. Can you see her now? – All right, thank you Ms Harrison.'

(to the visitor): 'Ms Harrison will be with you in about ten minutes, Mrs Hotch. Will that be all right? Take a seat please. Would you like a cup of coffee or tea while you are waiting?'

Helping visitors to find their way
When a visitor comes to see someone for the first time, accompany them to the right place. If this is not possible, ask the person who is expecting them to meet them in the reception area, or give them at least clear instructions.

DEALING WITH TRESPASSERS

If you see someone in the storeroom or in the offices who is not wearing a visitor's badge and whom you don't know, you should challenge them – politely, of course.

Challenge them even if they wear a workman's outfit or a uniform, or if they treat you in an arrogant way.

'Excuse me madam/sir, may I help you?' is the correct and polite way. Nobody can take this as an insult. But once they have explained who they are, you should still ask for credentials. Don't take their word that they are here to repair the toilets or that they are a plain-clothes police inspector.

If their response does not satisfy you, they are trespassers. You should ask them politely but firmly to leave the building. If they ignore your request, or become nasty, ask a colleague for help. If necessary, call the police.

COMMUNICATING WITH COLLEAGUES

Imagine you find a note on your desk, saying something like: 'John – please phone Sue.'

You know several people called Sue – there's your girlfriend, your cousin, the tutor at your evening drama class, the colleague who is off sick, the sales rep who called yesterday and the customer who sometimes phones with queries.

Whom do you phone? You could ask the person who wrote the note, but you don't know who it was. The handwriting is awful, so it could be your colleague Brian. Brian remembers that there was a phone call from a woman: 'I think someone from a company, she sounded official.'

So maybe it's Sue Singer, the sales rep. But where's her number? You look up her company in the *Yellow Pages*, but when you dial the number, you are told that Sue is out for the day, seeing customers. You have no idea what she wants.

How much quicker could you have acted if the note read: '20/9/XX, 9.30 am. Message for John: Sue Singer of Saul Ltd phoned. She has the information you requested about folk music CDs. Please phone her today before 2.30, or tomorrow, on tel. 0000/00000. Brian.'

There are different ways of talking to colleagues, for example:

- instructing
- reporting
- requesting
- ordering
- discussing

- enquiring
- informing.

Instructions and orders

While you are a trainee, you are more likely to receive orders than to give them. But you may be giving instructions. For example, you may explain to a work-experience person how to build a display unit, or to a new colleague how to receive visitors.

Your instructions must be clear. Repeat them if necessary, and encourage the person to ask questions. Explain not only what to do and how, but why it is done in this way.

If you receive instructions or orders, don't be afraid to ask the person to repeat or explain something in more detail. Repeat complicated instructions aloud, or write them down.

Requests

You request colleagues to lend you a hand when you can't do something alone, to help you when you are busy, or when you need their advice, or if something needs doing which is their job rather than yours. Always phrase your requests politely, maybe as a question, and add the word please: 'Mike, could you just show this lady where to find the washing powder?', 'Miss Turner, I'm afraid I still don't know how to do this properly. Could you show me again, please?'

A question gives the chance to say 'no'. But if you have to refuse a request, explain why. 'I'm sorry, John. I'm very busy today. But I could help you tomorrow.'

Reports

A report is a formal communication, usually to a manager or supervisor, or an outside authority. It often includes facts, figures and observations. It is a good idea to make a report in writing, or to take written notes with you when you make it.

Discussions

You discuss matters with a group of colleagues to pool your ideas – for example, how to make your shelves more accessible, or how to save energy. It can also be just two colleagues discussing something: 'John, I have this problem and I need your opinion, but please don't tell anybody.'

Of course you must keep discussions, reports and requests which were made in confidence confidential.

BUILDING GOOD RELATIONSHIPS WITH COLLEAGUES

You spend several hours every day with your colleagues, possibly more than with your wife, husband, boyfriend, girlfriend or parents, so it is important that you get on well. The easiest way to make people like you is to be courteous and helpful, and to smile a lot.

Dealing with problems

It is natural that some people like each other less than others. Not everyone can like every other person. This is not necessarily a problem. If it is just a clash of personalities, simply accept that you are different. Treat each other politely, in a purely professional way, and keep away from each other when possible.

Never show your dislike for another person in front of customers, or quarrel and argue on the sales floor, however justified your anger is.

Maybe there is a concrete reason why you dislike a person. In this case it is better to tackle the underlying problem before you build up aggression against him or her.

Most problems can be solved by talking. Whatever gets on your nerves – the use of swearwords, sexist or racist jokes, interrupting you whenever you say something – let the person know (diplomatically if possible). They are probably not even aware that they offend you, and will probably be willing to change or at least modify their behaviour.

Other situations which can put a strain on your relationship with colleagues may affect your work or the business. Perhaps you have seen a colleague stealing goods from the storeroom, or you know that she is reading comics in the ladies' when others are busy working.

First, you must tell the colleague that you disapprove of their behaviour. Explain why you think it is a problem. Choose a quiet, private situation for this discussion.

If they don't change their behaviour, it can be necessary to make a report to the manager. Speak calmly, in a matter-of-fact way, without showing personal dislike. State the facts. You can also mention assumptions and your reasons for them, but don't present your assumptions as facts.

CASE STUDIES

John's telephone manner gets results

Pete Polter wants to buy the latest CD by the Pink Poodles. He lives in a small village, and the nearest record shop is Music Plus in Poodletown. Before taking the bus into town, he decides to ring Music Plus.

He dials. The phone keeps ringing for a long time. Finally someone responds 'Eh? Hello? Who's that there?'

Pete asks: 'Is that Music Plus? Yes? I just wonder if you have the CD "Paranoid Parachute" by the Pink Poodles?'

The person on the other end replies: 'No idea. It's not my job, you know, I'm only the trainee. Don't think there are any, but maybe. I'll have to look upstairs, or maybe in the stockroom. There's a lot of CDs there which haven't been unpacked.'

Pete hears nothing for a long time. He assumes the person has gone upstairs, and he keeps waiting. After six minutes, the line goes dead.

Next, he dials another record shop, Off The Record. After three rings, he hears a friendly voice: 'Good morning, this is Off The Record, John Anderson speaking. How may I help you?'

Pete explains what he wants. John Anderson replies: 'It is not on the shelves. But we have just received a new delivery. If it is a new CD, it may be among them. I will have to check in the stockroom. May I ring you back in about five minutes? – Can you please repeat your name? What is your phone number please? Thank you, Mr Polter, I'll get back to you soon.'

A few minutes later, the phone rings. 'Hello, is that Pete Polter? This is John Anderson from Off The Record. Yes, we have the new CD here.'

John Anderson repeats the name of the band and the title of the CD, and mentions the price. 'Shall I put one aside for you? When do you think you will come? – That's fine, Mr Polter. I'll tell my colleagues that you'll be calling this afternoon. Thank you, goodbye Mr Polter.'

It is easy to guess which record shop Pete Polter will be visiting in the afternoon, where he will buy his records in future, and which shop he will recommend to his friends.

In fact, the competitors, Music Plus, had the requested CD in stock, too, at a much lower price. But after his experience on the phone, Pete Polter will not even bother to find that out.

Rebecca considers confidential information

A university student calls at the shop. 'I'm working on a degree project on trends in the fashion industry,' she explains. 'Can you answer a few questions?'

'I'll certainly help if I can,' replies Rebecca. She has a look at the list of questions. Among others, she wants to know how many items of clothing Streetwise sells per day, how old the average customer is, which is the bestselling item, which size is most in demand, and the names and addresses of some customers.

'Well, I can answer some of your questions,' says Rebecca. 'Our typical customers are young women in the late teens and early twenties, and most of them are wearing a size twelve. These white cotton blouses with lace collars are selling very well. If you need figures and statistics, I suggest you talk to our manager Miss Turner. She'll be back tomorrow afternoon. Shall I tell her that you'll be calling? Perhaps you can bring a letter from your university or some similar credentials?'

'And will she give me addresses of customers?' asks the student.

'I'm afraid we can't give you customer information, that's confidential. But I'll think about how we can help you in this matter. I'm sure I can come up with an idea by tomorrow.'

Linda relays a message

It is 12 noon. Linda's colleague, Carol, is putting on her coat. 'I must dash, my husband's waiting. If Mr Knight comes − you know, that funny old chap with the green hat who is always cracking jokes and whose ties always have stains, nice chap really though − will you please give him the plastic bag under the cashtill? Not the first checkout, the third from the right − no wait, it's the fourth, anyway, there's a carrier bag with his shopping, I think he wanted to go to the bookshop or something. He's paid for the potatoes or whatever it is, some vegetables anyway, and he said he'd probably come around noon. Can you do that? Thanks, bye.'

'Just a moment, while I write this down,' replies Linda, who is concerned that she may not remember the essential details. 'Mr Knight with a green hat, will come around noon to collect a carrier bag full of vegetables for which he has already paid. The bag is under the fourth checkout desk. Is this right? Thanks, I'll see to it. Have a nice lunch.'

POINTS FOR DISCUSSION

1. Imagine you are John at the record shop. You find that you don't have the record in stock. You phone Peter Polter, but there's an answerphone. Write down the wording of the message you are going to leave.

2. Imagine you are Rebecca at the fashion shop. A reporter is writing an article about the latest fashion trends for young working women, for the lifestyle pages of the local newspaper. The manager is away on holiday, and you are the only member of staff available for interview.

   Your shop's policy is to keep good relations with the press. You know your manager would be happy for you to give an interview about fashion and sales in general terms, because this means excellent free publicity for the shop.

   In the absence of the manager, she interviews you briefly about the clothes in stock, which clothes sell best, and a forecast for the spring fashion.

   The reporter asks you for the phone numbers of some regular customers, because she wants to interview 'ordinary' people. Your shop has a file with the names, addresses, telephone numbers and buying preferences of regular customers.

   You don't want to breach the confidentiality of this information, but you want to help the reporter as much as possible. There is no senior member of staff available to ask for advice. The reporter needs the information within an hour because she has to work to a tight deadline.

   How do you solve the dilemma?

3. Imagine you are Linda at the supermarket. It's time for your own lunch break now, but Mr Knight still has not come. You want to give the message about the carrier back to another colleague, but he plans to leave for lunch soon, too.

   You decide to give him a written note, which he can pass on to whoever will be in the shop at the time.

   Write that note.

4. Design a telephone note form for the shop where you are working. If a special form exists already, design one which is even more practical.

5. In the shop in which you are working, who communicates with whom, when and in which way? Think of at least one example for a report, in order, a request, an instruction, and a discussion.

6. Over the last week, how many visitors came to your shop? Who were they?

7. Imagine you are Linda at Westmore's. You observe that one colleague, Carol, is making deliberate mistakes at the cashpoint. Whenever her friends or family do any shopping, she keys in much lower prices, for example, £0.99 instead of £9.99.

   You wait and observe until you are sure that your suspicion is justified. Then you take Carol to the side and tell her that you are concerned about this. Her behaviour is costing the shop a lot of money. You mention that the manager is already suspecting the sales staff which is creating an awkward atmosphere. But Carol hardly listens to what you say. You point out that you will have to report her to the manager, but she tells you to mind your own business.

   You decide to talk to the manager. Write down what you are going to say.

8. You used to get on well with your colleague, Marion. But recently she has changed. She has become moody and snappish, not only with you, but with all the other colleagues. She appears tired, her hands are trembling, she is short-tempered and cannot concentrate on a task, and she is sometimes unfriendly to customers. The manager has already had a serious word with her, but to no avail.

   At first you thought the change in her personality had been brought about by personal problems: she is going through a messy divorce, her mother has died, her teenage son has repeatedly been caught stealing, she was evicted from her flat and lost her driving licence – all in the last three months. You feel sorry for her.

   Then you discover by coincidence that the thermos flask she brings to work every day is not filled with tea but with neat whisky. At a staff party, she drinks not one but seven glasses of wine. She may be an alcoholic.

   What will you do in this situation?

9. Imagine you are Rebecca. You observe how the assistant manager, Mrs Baldock, criticises colleagues in front of customers. She even shouts at the work-experience person who has made a mistake, with a dozen customers standing around and listening. If a customer asks a question she considers stupid, she makes sarcastic comments which really embarrass the customers. You have noticed that several customers have not returned to the shop after Mrs Baldock embarrassed them.

   When you try to criticise Mrs Baldock, she only says: 'What do you

know about business? You are only the trainee. I've been in retailing
for thirty-five years. Don't try to tell me how to treat customers and
staff.'

You are concerned that the shop is losing customers rapidly. What
can you do?

9
Good Housekeeping

Cleaning and tidying up is probably not your favourite aspect of retail work, and maybe your store employs cleaners anyway. But there is always some cleaning and tidying work to do for sales staff, for example removing the broken glass bottle or the banana peel from the floor.

A clean and tidy shop looks neat, is accessible to customers, makes work easier for the staff, and is safe to use for everyone.

Remember to:

- Carry out emergency cleaning at once (*eg* broken glass, spilled poisonous liquids).

- Do non-urgent cleaning and housekeeping during slack periods, with as little disturbance to customers as possible.

- Store away all cleaning materials after use.

DEALING WITH DAMAGED STOCK

Stock can get damaged by accident, or because staff or customers handle the goods carelessly.

Examples

- An assistant drops a heavy box with glass tumblers. One of them gets cracked, the others are still in good order.

- The basement where clothes are stored is flooded after heavy rainfalls. The clothes are soaked and soiled. They can be washed and dried, but cannot be sold as 'new'.

- A silk dress has a make-up stain after a customer has tried it on and left the shop.

Don't sell damaged goods at full price, otherwise your shop gets a poor reputation, and you will spend much time giving refunds. You can do either of the following:

- Mark them down (selling them at a reduced rate).

- Sell them to a specialist dealer who markets damaged stock.

USING RESOURCES ECONOMICALLY

Materials such as carrier bags, self-adhesive tape and wrapping paper may just cost a penny a time, but if they are used a lot, the costs soon mount up.

Would you like a bag?
Three reasons for using plastic carrier bags are:

1. They make it easier for the customer to carry their purchases home.

2. They show that the goods have been paid for.

3. They are good advertisements if they are printed with the shop's colours, logo or name.

Three reasons against using plastic carrier bags are:

1. They cost money.

2. They usually get binned as soon as the customer gets home.

3. Their production and disposal damages the environment.

Unless your shop has its own policy for carrier bags, ask 'Would you like a bag?' The customer can reply 'Yes, please.' or 'No thanks, I've brought my own.'
    It helps to have bags in various sizes, as well as special wrapping or purpose-made bags for special goods, handy at the checkout.

CUTTING DOWN ON THE PHONE BILL

The phone bills of some stores are enormous. Possible ways of reducing these are:

- Prepare what you are going to say before dialling.

- Making phone calls only during cheap rate periods, *eg* weekends and evenings. However, this is not practical for most shops.

- Fit dialling locks, or give access to authorised employees only, or record every single call made, or ask BT for an itemised bill, to stop employees making private phone calls.

- Charge employees for private phone calls.

- Install a pay phone on the premises for staff use.

CUTTING DOWN ON ADMINISTRATIVE COSTS

Some companies lose a lot of money because dishonest staff steal stationery and stamps, and use the photocopier for private purposes. To prevent this, some shops keep the stationery cupboard locked and appoint a senior member of staff to keep a list of who have received what. However, this is not always economical. The senior employee's time may cost more than the disappearing pencils are worth.

Other shops fit a lock to the photocopier. Only authorised staff have a key. Some use code numbers to give access to the photocopier.

Remember that using the photocopier for private purposes without permission is theft. The same applies if you take home the occasional envelope or pencil. You may end up losing your job and ruining your career prospects over this.

SAVING ENERGY

Economic lighting
Good light is important for safety and comfort. Don't try to switch lights on and off all the time; it won't save any money.

But it pays to switch off all lights in rooms which are seldom used.

Out of trading hours, you should keep only the security lights on. Consider buying low-energy light bulbs and tubes. Check and clean bulbs and tubes regularly, replace those which are not working properly.

Reducing the heating bill

If the heating bills are high, shopkeepers should consider the following:

- Fit thermostats and set them at the lowest acceptable temperature.

- Reduce temperatures when it gets warmer, *eg* in the afternoons, or when the weather changes.

- Use timers to heat the building at a time when electricity charges are lower, but only if this is practical.

- Close the doors in the storage and office areas to save energy. Your shop's policy may demand that you keep the shop doors open.

- Keep the windows closed. Open them wide every couple of hours for ten minutes or so to get fresh air. This is better than keeping one window open a little all the time.

Stopping money going down the drain

A dripping water tap can cost a lot of money. If you notice a dripping tap, get the washers replaced or the tap repaired.

ENVIRONMENTALLY FRIENDLY – AND PROFITABLE

Most shops pay a waste-collection company to collect the waste regularly.

Try to dispose of waste material in an environmentally friendly way. You can take paper, cardboard, old brochures, empty bottles and damaged textiles to the nearest paper, bottle or textile banks. If you collect a lot of waste paper, you may be able to sell it and earn some extra money for the shop. Some waste-collection companies also pay for other types of waste, for example for certain chemicals and plastics.

CASE STUDIES

Rebecca assesses the damage

After sudden heavy rainfall, the basement at Streetwise is flooded. Staff salvage the goods stored there. However, many items have been soaked in muddy water and are dirty. The manager, Miss Turner, decides to sell the goods at a reduced price.

Luckily, the shop has insurance which will pay for the losses. However, the insurance company needs detailed information on which items have been damaged, and how much the prices will have to be reduced. Miss Turner asks Rebecca Smith to put the information together.

As there are several hundred soiled items, Rebecca wonders if there is a systematic way of going about this task.

John helps cut the bills

A comparison between several branches of Off The Record shows that the shop has proportionally higher telephone and electricity bills. The manager would like to reduce these costs, but can't find the time to work out a practical plan. John decides to draw up a list of suggestions.

Westmore's Supermarket goes green

Many customers at Westmores show increasing concern about the environment. The management decides to give the shop an environmentally friendly, 'green' image, and ask the staff for suggestions.

Linda has been waiting for this opportunity. She has noticed how much potentially recyclable waste gets binned. She has suggestions how to turn waste into money, and she has several 'green' ideas which involve the customers, too.

POINTS FOR DISCUSSION

1. Imagine you are Rebecca. Develop a system with which to record the damaged items.

   There are several ways of going about this. Decide on a method which you find practical. It must give your manager, as well as the insurance assessor, a clear idea of the number of damaged items, the type of damaged items, a description of the damage, the purchase price, the intended retail price, and the suggested mark-down price. You can add additional information if you think it would be useful.

   Design a suitable form to fill in, or write down how you propose to go about the task.

2. Imagine you are John. Produce a written report about how energy

could be saved, and how phone bills could be reduced. You can use your own imagination to describe what is wrong at Off The Record, and what can be done about it.

3. Imagine you are Linda. At present, all waste is stored in one large container at the rear of the shop, and collected three times a week. Westmore's pay a hefty bill for it. Most of the waste is cardboard, polystyrene and plastic. Make suggestions what to do with the waste. You may need more specific advice about environmentally-friendly and profitable waste disposal. Where would you turn to get the information you need?

Remember that it is even more environmentally-friendly and profitable to prevent unnecessary waste in the first place.

Think of several other ideas how to be environmentally-friendly, and how to create a 'green' image. Possible areas to consider are: carrier bags, letterheads, brochures, stocking environmentally-friendly/ organically-grown/fairly-traded goods, competitions/activities for school children, a waste collection/recycling point for customers. The more suggestions you can make, the better.

Prepare a written, structured report to present to the management.

4. Write a report for the shop where you are working. You can choose a subject from the list below. But let your supervisor know that you are preparing a report. He or she may have some suggestions, too. Obviously, you must research what the current situation is, and which facilities exist locally.
'Ways of reducing the phone bills'
'Ways of saving energy'
'Ways of reducing our stationery costs'
'How to be more environmentally friendly'
'Avoiding, reducing and recycling waste'.

10
Accepting Deliveries

Like so many things that we have to do, if we prepare properly and approach the job in an organised fashion there is less likelihood of mistakes and the whole process will be without problems.

There is responsibility when accepting deliveries in the same way as there is responsibility when handling cash, so you will want to do it right.

RECEIVING INCOMING STOCK

It is most usual for deliveries to be on a particular day of the week, especially if large amounts of stock are delivered at one time. So it will be easy to anticipate some of the things that can be done to make the process run smoothly. The first thing to do is to prepare the area where the stock will be received.

- Will you need to make extra space available?
- If the sales floor will be affected, how can you minimise the disruption?
- Will you need any lifting equipment or trolleys?
- Will you need help from another person to carry heavy loads?
- What other equipment will be necessary *eg* scissors, tools, rails?

When the lorry arrives, the driver will have a delivery note which will usually identify the number of pieces which are to be delivered. This can be the number of cartons, the number of bags, the number of crates – whichever is appropriate to the type of goods you will be receiving.

It is essential that these are checked, agreed and signed for before the driver leaves.

UNPACKING THE STOCK

The next process, is to unpack the stock and prepare it for the stockroom or the shopfloor. It may be necessary to unwrap or unpack the goods from the outer packaging and this must be done effectively and safely, disposing of the unwanted packaging materials as soon as possible.

When you have unpacked the stock you will be able to check off the delivery in detail against an assignment note or invoice. You will be looking in detail to make sure that:

- the correct number of items is present
- the sizes are correct
- all the parts are intact
- the colours are as stated
- there is no damage to the items which could have happened in transit.

It may be that the types of goods that you are dealing with do actually stay partly wrapped or packaged for sale so you do not see the item itself. You will still be looking for warning signs of what may be damaged goods. For example, leakages, odours, torn outer packaging or even, in some cases, a change of colour will warn you that the goods may not be of the standard required.

You may find it easier to check off a delivery note with another person. If one person calls out the items on the delivery note and another checks off the actual goods, it is a methodical approach which is quick and accurate.

Dresses	Streetwise plc					Delivery note
Style No	Colour	10	12	14	16	Total
1476	Blue	2	4	4	2	12
1479	Blue	6	10	8	6	30
1623	Red	4	7	7	5	23
1623	Blue	7	10	10	5	32
1594	Green	4	8	8	6	26
		23	39	37	24	123

Fig. 15. Checking-off deliveries.

DEALING WITH DISCREPANCIES OR DAMAGED GOODS

A delivery or assignment note is the administrative method of recording stock going into your store. If you find that the details on the delivery note do not correspond with the actual items received, then you will have to record this in accordance with your own company's procedures. These differences can be a greater number or a smaller number than stated or items which are different to the delivery note. It will also apply to items which are damaged and therefore cannot be sold. The stock records have to be adjusted so that the accurate information is credited to your store.

Make sure that you understand the correct procedures for doing this and that you take any necessary action quickly. You will need to know:

- the paperwork necessary to record discrepancies
- what to do with damaged stock
- what to do with contaminated stock
- what to do if the stock has become hazardous
- the company policy regarding selling damaged stock at discounted prices.

To conclude the process of receiving the delivery you will need to know the correct location for the stock once you have dealt with the administration. Does it go on to the shop floor or does it go into the stockroom? Does this apply to some of the delivery or all of it?

When you have taken the stock to the correct place you can review the

DRESSES	STREETWISE plc								ERROR REPORT
	INVOICE				ACTUAL			TOTAL DIFF	COMMENTS
STYLE NO	10	12	14	16	10	12	14	16	
1623	4	7	7	5	4	7	6	5	1 short	
1594	4	8	8	6	4	8	8	8	2 over	
1476	2	4	4	2	2	4	6	—	—	SIZE ONLY

Fig. 16. An example of a form recording discrepancies.

delivery area. Is all the equipment that you have had to use back where it belongs? Has all surplus wrapping and packing materials been disposed of? Is it now restored to the way it was before the delivery?

CASE STUDIES

Dealing with the delivery

Rebecca was helping with the delivery. All the staff had come in a little early so that the new stock could be marked off and dealt with before the shop got really busy. She was getting used to the routine and had helped get some spare hanging rails in place near the back door so that the delivery could go straight on to them. They also had scissors and the error report book.

The delivery had just arrived and the manager had checked with the driver that they had twelve hanging bags, fifteen large polythene bags and two boxes. She signed his docket and he went on his way.

The first thing to do now was to get the clear polythene covers off the hanging stock. This was done carefully so that the stock underneath did not get damaged. Then the polythene was taken away as it is very slippery when left on the carpet. Rebecca was then ready to check off against the invoice which her manager had given her. She was doing this with Jayne. Rebecca was calling out and Jayne was checking off.

'Style 1475, blue,' said Rebecca. Jayne found the entry on the invoice.

'Eight size ten, sixteen size twelve, twelve size fourteen, and six size sixteen' said Rebecca counting and gradually moving the stock along the rail as she dealt with it. Jayne confirmed that that was what was on the invoice and so they went on to the next style. They did this until all the hanging stock was checked off.

Rebecca has also learnt the importance of new stock in the achievement of their sales targets. It was important to get a selection on to the shop floor as quickly as possible. She selected two of each size and colour and went and placed them on the shop floor in a prominent position. Then she and Jayne put the remainder away in the stockroom. They did this process for all the hanging stock.

Meanwhile, two other members of staff were emptying the large polythene bags. These had contained blouses and jumpers, but the process of checking off was the same.

Finally, Rebecca and Jayne had to open the two boxes. In there were handbags and other accessories. These were smaller items and needed a lot of concentration so the manager had said they could take their time. The new fashion stock was out and that was the main thing.

When they were checking some belts, Rebecca and Jayne found that they had got twenty-seven brown and thirty black. There should have been thirty of each. Then they found that they had seven black handbags and three brown when in fact the invoice said ten black.

Rebecca knew that she had to do error reports for both of these. Even though the handbags were the correct number and price, the information as far as stock control was concerned had to be amended.

Dealing with discrepancies

John had just finished putting the new stock away after the delivery had been marked off. There was some which had gone into the stockroom and some which had gone on to the shop floor. He made sure that he had dealt with it correctly by taking the tapes and CDs out of the boxes before putting the boxes on display.

Now he had to deal with some differences that they had discovered when checking off. He had left it until all the delivery had been done and the shop floor was tidy and the new stock was in place. He did this so that all the discrepancies could be dealt with together and also it was not delaying the new stock getting on to the shop floor.

He went into the office with the invoices and the notes he had made about the discrepancies. John knew it was important to be accurate so he closed the door so that he could give his full attention to the paperwork.

Completing the error reports was something John had only just learned to do so he had to think carefully about the correct procedure.

Having thought it through he realised that it was logical really. The invoice was a computerised printout of what should have been sent to the shop. Unfortunately, however, someone had made a mistake when putting it together. So John now had to compile the error report in such a way that the correct information could be put back into the computer. The error report book for Off The Record had been designed to do just that. John had to supply the details of

- what they should have received
- what they actually received
- the difference, plus or minus.

Putting it this way made it easy for John to follow and meant that when the information was received at the warehouse it could not be misinterpreted by the computer operator who would key in the revised figures.

John also knew that he had to fill in an error report to correct the stock records even if the numbers were correct but the details were wrong regarding titles and so on.

Dealing with damaged stock

Linda had been asked to come in and do some overtime as they were short staffed at Westmores due to holidays. She didn't mind and she would also be helping with the deliveries – something she did not usually do, so it would be a change.

She was checking off the crates of wine with Graham and then two of the lads were moving them away to the stockroom. They had done quite a lot when Linda noticed that the next crate had a dark stain on the outside.

'What's that mark?' she said to Graham.

'Looks like some of the wine has spilled,' he replied.

They looked more closely and then looked at the bottles, but there wasn't a broken one.

'Must be something spilled on to it from the outside,' said Graham picking up his pen to carry on checking off.

'Just a minute,' said Linda. 'This seal appears to be broken. I didn't notice at first, but it must have seeped out over a period of time. What shall we do about it?'

'It can't be that bad,' said Graham. 'We can still check it off.'

But Linda wasn't happy with that and said, 'Let's find out for sure from Mr Turner. Wines and Spirits is his department and he will know what to do.'

POINTS FOR DISCUSSION

1. How many important points regarding health and safety when dealing with deliveries can you think of?

2. What are the considerations regarding care of the stock and preventing damage when unpacking the deliveries?

3. Why is it important to make an error report for stock which is the wrong colour? Can you think of a situation where sales in a fashion shop could be affected if blue belts are delivered instead of red?

4. If the error was an over delivery, does this have to be reported?

5. What might have been the consequences if Linda had not asked for the advice of Mr Turner when the seal was broken?

6. Find out what are the procedures for dealing with damaged stock in your shop. Does it go back to the warehouse, the manufacturer or the supplier? Does it get disposed of? Are there special procedures?

11
Handling Stock

In an earlier chapter we talked about stock knowledge and how a sales assistant should know all about the stock in the shop. If they know about the features and benefits they will be able to help a customer choose exactly what is right for them.

In the same way a good sales assistant will know how to look after the stock before it is sold and how to store it to the best advantage. This will be for the benefit of the organisation and for the benefit of the stock.

Let's look first at how the organisation can benefit from good stock control and storage.

THE STOCKROOM

The layout of the stockroom is almost as important as the layout of the shop floor. It will make stock replenishment easier if the stockroom is tidy and the layout is easy to keep to.

The layout of the stockroom will make sure that each type of merchandise or stock is kept in an easily identifiable area. The amount of space allocated to each area will also reflect the amount of stock holding. It is no good allowing too much space for one type of merchandise when another is so cramped that the stock may get damaged.

The shelves and rails should be filled with stock in a way that the stock can easily be selected when needed on the shop floor. Do you remember how we talked about merchandising in an earlier chapter? There may be times when you have a line of merchandise that is selling very quickly and you will need to refill the shop floor on a regular basis. You will not want to waste valuable time in the stockroom looking for best sellers and lose the opportunity to make some extra sales because you cannot find the right stock.

Have you ever asked to try on a pair of shoes you have seen in the window of a shop and when the sales assistant has gone to find a pair in the stockroom, you cannot understand why they are taking so long? Just at the moment you are beginning to wonder if they have gone for a tea-break they reappear looking harassed and frustrated. A customer will not always wait and anyway it is so much easier for the sales assistant when the layout of the stockroom is easy to understand.

Organising the stockroom

Some simple rules are:

- Keep it tidy – it will be a safer place too!

- Store items by keeping the same type of merchandise together.

- Make sure the sizes or code numbers are visible.

- Make sure the allocation of space is appropriate.

- Use the correct storage equipment for the type of merchandise.

If you follow those rules you will be able to help the customer quickly and efficiently with stock that is in good condition and therefore, more likely to give satisfaction.

You may be required to count or record stock-levels and you will need to know whether the items are recorded by packs, by single units, by dozens or by weight.

There are two main reasons why it is important to know how much stock is in the stockroom. The first of these is security. The management need to know if any stock is missing so that they can monitor the situation and prevent it happening again. The figures which will provide this information are taken from the original delivery, minus the number sold. This will show the amount currently held in the stockroom. If there is a discrepancy then it may indicate that there has been either a mistake in the recording of the delivery, a mistake in the recording of the sale or worse still a theft of merchandise from the stockroom.

The second reason for counting the stock is to monitor the levels of particular items and make sure that there are plenty of items that are selling well but not overstocks of slow lines. Sales will be lost if the customer wants current trends or seasonal goods when the stockroom is full of out-of-date items.

Some out-of-date items can also be a hazard if they are perishable.

DEALING WITH ITEMS THAT NEED SPECIAL STORAGE OR HANDLING

You may need to be conscious of hygiene in your place of work. This applies to your own personal hygiene and also the special requirements for food and medical supplies. If you need to wear protective hairnets or hats, make sure that all of your hair is enclosed. You will have ample provision for washing your hands when dealing with food or some medical products. Any other protective clothing or equipment will be made available to you so make sure you know what is required and where the necessary things are stored.

There may be a need for special attention to safety if you are dealing with inflammable goods. These must be stored where there is no risk of fire.

Items of high value will also have to be treated as a special case. These may be a high cash value but they may also be a high risk value such as cigarettes or alcohol. They should be stored in a safe area where the risk of theft can be reduced.

HYGIENIC FOOD-HANDLING

Foodstuffs must be treated with the described high level of hygiene already mentioned. But you must also learn about contamination and the correct temperatures at which certain foods must be stored.

Make a list of types of food kept and sold in your shop. For each product group, complete the following checklist:

1. Does the product need to be kept at a specific temperature?

2. Are there other specific conditions, for example, must the product be kept out of direct light, or in dry conditions?

3. Is it safe to display the product open, or must it be wrapped at all times?

4. How long can we keep it in the storeroom or in the shop?

5. Which are the specific dangers to this product (*eg*, salmonella, mould . . .)

6. How, and how often, do we check if the product is still in good condition? Goods may leave the supplier in perfect condition but can become spoiled by careless retailers.

7. If the food has 'gone off', how do we dispose of it safely?

Keeping food fresh

All items of food need your attention, to prevent them from perishing or becoming health hazards. For some products, the list of rules can be long. You may wonder why shops have to follow so many rules in handling food, when the average householder is able to ignore them all. It does not make sense if you keep the fresh meat in the shop clean, wrapped, at the right temperature and under constant supervision, if the householder then takes it home, unwraps it, touches it with dirty fingers and leaves it in the open, exposed to dust and flies.

The reason, however, is simple. If food gets contaminated in a private household, it's just one family who suffers the effects. If there is negligence in a store, hundreds of people may be affected by salmonella or food poisoning.

Some rules to remember

The following rules will help ensure that the food in your shop stays fresh:

- Try not to handle unwrapped food as well as money. If you are making sandwiches for your customers, arrange for a colleague to take payment. If this is not possible, wash your hands each time after taking the money and before handling the food.

- If you sell bakery products or other open foodstuffs, check the shelves and window displays frequently for dead flies, especially on hot days.

- Check your displays and stocks of fresh fruit and vegetables regularly, especially when the weather is changing. Fruit which looked fine a couple of hours ago may suddenly 'go off', and infect neighbouring food items.

- If any item of food looks suspicious, be ruthless. 'If in doubt, throw it out!'

- Check your freezer chest regularly. Each chest has a maximum filling line. Don't be tempted to pile the goods higher; the temperature above the line is not sufficient. Customers often move packets from one pile to another, not knowing about the maximum filling line.

- Keep an eye on all freezer and refrigerator units. Customers who are in a hurry may not close them properly, which means the temperature levels are not maintained.

- Never leave items which are past their 'best before' or 'sell-by' dates in the shelves. Don't try to cheat the customers by just sticking a price label on the sell-by date. If they notice it, they will be angry. If they eat the product, they may fall ill and hold the shop responsible.

CASE STUDIES

Linda deals with deteriorated stock

Linda is helping to stack some of the shelves in Westmore's Supermarket. She is on the vegetable counter, dealing with some punnets of strawberries. She notices the sell-by date is different on some of them, so she makes sure that she puts those with the later date at the back of the shelves.

There are seven punnets that have strawberries in that have become squashed and are beginning to go mouldy. She takes those off display and puts them to one side to dispose of later.

Good stockroom layout

John was busy in the stockroom in Off The Record. He had gone in there to find a record for a customer and it was not immediately obvious where it was. In fact, he eventually had to go to the customer and apologise because they were out of stock.

When the shop was quieter and he had some time, John went into the stockroom and took a critical look round. There did not seem to be any system and it was difficult to see exactly what was there.

'Can I do some work to reorganise the stockroom?' he asked Mr Gregory.

'Yes, if you think it will be worth it,' he replied.

The first thing John did was to do a superficial job in tidying up. Then he could see what needed doing. He sorted the different types of goods into their own areas. Then he sorted the types of music within those areas. He found quite a few video tapes that he knew were not selling well. He made a note of how many there were and the details, including the selling price.

Then he had a look to see how many records and CDs there were that were in the top 100. He found one of those he had been looking for earlier. The next thing he did was to look at the sales figures for the last week.

'Can I make a suggestion, Mr Gregory. The stockroom is very full up although I have now tidied it so it doesn't look quite so bad. But we could do with some more space for the top 100. We don't have enough stock to meet our sales targets but I feel sure we could sell them if we had the right stock.'

'What would you like to do?' asked Mr Gregory.

'Can we reduce the price on that old stock and get rid of it. That would give us the space we need. I'd like to get on to the supplier to increase our delivery this week so that we will have a good supply in for next Saturday. We can always sell a lot on Saturday if only we have the stock in the stockroom.'

Mr Gregory was very pleased that John had done this exercise. It showed initiative on his part – and it would increase sales! John was pleased too because he could see the results of his hard work.

Replenishing stock

Rebecca had noticed that the new line in tee-shirts that had come in yesterday was selling really fast. They were in a range of colours and sizes and she had paid attention to them this morning when she first arrived at work. She always made a point of looking at the new stock so that she could improve her stock-knowledge – she liked to know about everything in the shop! Not only was she better able to help customers but she loved looking at the new styles and colours.

So she had noticed that there were a lot of the new tee-shirts then. Now at just after 11 o'clock the rails were getting empty and she knew that it was important to fill up before the busy lunch-time period.

Rebecca went and got a piece of paper to make some notes on and listed how many she had in each size and colour on the rails. She felt sure that it would be better if they had three size ten, three size twelve and three size fourteen in blue, also in red and green. The black did not seem to be selling so well so two of each size would probably be enough.

Having made a list of what she had on the shop floor, Rebecca then worked out what she needed to fill up the rails to the required level. In the stockroom, she was able to quickly select the stock as they had been put on the shelves according to colour and size. She was back on the shop-floor in five minutes and was hanging the stock when her manager came over.

'I see you've just replenished the tee-shirts,' she said. 'I'd like you to keep an eye on those as I feel sure that we will need to get on to the warehouse for a repeat order. I don't want to miss out on some sales simply because we haven't got enough stock.'

As soon as the lunchtime was over, Rebecca checked on how many tee-shirts were on the rails again. She was amazed at how many had been sold and went through the same process to fill up the gaps. Rebecca then told her manager of the numbers that were left in the stockroom so that she could do a forecast of potential sales and make sure that she had enough stock to achieve her targets.

POINTS FOR DISCUSSION

1. Why is it important to put the stock with the later sell-by date at the back? What might be the result of selling food which has started to go mouldy?

2. How could John determine how much stock he would need to meet the sales targets? If the stock that was to be reduced was old, how could this be displayed to have the best impact?

3. The process Rebecca carried out with the tee-shirts is called 'proportionate display' which means displaying goods in the proportion that they are likely to sell. They were selling three of each colour compared to two of black. If you work in a fashion shop, it may be that you sell four small sizes compared to eight medium and two large. In a hardware store, it may be 40 watt bulbs compared to 60 watt and 100 watt. Look for examples of this in your shop and see if you could replenish the stock quickly and effectively if the need arose. Is the stockroom well laid out to help make this job simple and safe?

12
Looking to the Future

CHANGES IN RETAILING TODAY

There is nothing so constant as change.

This is a very true saying and those people who choose retailing for a career know this better than most. In fact, it is often the thing that makes retailing so enjoyable. The dynamism, the reactive response to trends, and the fickleness of the public are the challenges to the retailer.

However there are major changes that are taking place in retailing today. The first of these is technology. There are now very sophisticated methods for taking payments, recording sales and replenishing stock. These are computers which have replaced the electronic tills which were commonplace in the 1980s. The present day machines are just like tills to the customer but will also provide sales forecasts so that managers can determine the required stockholding in all the lines they sell. The machines can also provide trading patterns, *ie* the busiest time of the day, so that staffing levels can be worked out in order to give the best possible service. They can also provide complete reconciliations of cash and stock records at the end of the day. As a result, less staff are needed off the shop floor, thereby concentrating on providing more customer service.

Linked with the methods of payment is the increased activity of credit companies. Many stores offer their own credit card facilities although these are frequently administered by the major banks. The main reason for these cards is to encourage customer loyalty. If a man wants a new suit and he has a store card for a particular outfitter, that is where he is going to go. But it can also provide better customer service by giving the customer the opportunity to budget easily. Another activity of the credit companies is in their own interest – and that is to reduce fraud. The cards now have holograms on them to reduce the likelihood of misuse or theft and currently the credit card companies are considering photographs on the cards to be even more effective in the drive against crime.

Another new development is the presentation of 'lifestyles'. The concept of the customer shopping according to their lifestyle was a product of the eighties and has been widely adopted. Habitat probably was one of the innovators of this concept but it has been adopted by others. In more recent years, Laura Ashley became known as a successful women's fashion chain. Their customer was very clearly defined – so much so that it became easy to imagine the customer in her home. What sort of decor would she favour? Laura Ashley were then able to branch into home furnishings and satisfy their customers in a new range of products. So the demographic group is targeted with a wide range of products to match a lifestyle.

Mail order is now being offered as an additional customer service by many retailers who have traditionally traded from High Street sites. This is a trend that has developed as a result of social changes. It satisfies two needs. On the one hand it makes shopping easier for those people who work, especially the increasing number of women following careers. And on the other hand, mail order provides opportunities for credit shopping.

Large stores are opening in out of town shopping precincts and this is having an effect on the local 'corner shop'. Being able to buy in substantial quantities means that the large chain can offer very competitive prices to their customers. In addition, we become more continental in our approach and we expect to be able to shop later in the evening and on Sundays. It is more common for the family to go shopping together on a Sunday and to fill the car with groceries and other items.

The drive to give a better service and thereby beat the competitors is what brings about these changes. A retailer who increases sales by a percentage which is similar to the rate of inflation is in fact only standing still. The company must increase their sales by more than inflation in order to reinvest and grow.

Increasing sales is achieved by the hard work of effective sales assistants who know how to give good customer service in every sense of the word. It also means being aware of opportunities and making changes in order to meet customer demands.

CASE STUDIES

Being taken over

Rebecca was very concerned about some rumours she had heard that her shop was going to be part of a big chain. She didn't like the sound of that too much and was worried about being made redundant.

'What will happen to us?' she asked her manager one morning.

'We shall have to wait and see. I don't know any more than you.'

In fact, the news broke quite soon and all the rumours about a takeover had been true. The result was immediate in so far as changes were going to take place in the way the shop was run but it appeared that there were not going to be any redundancies.

Rebecca had to go away on a two-day training course to learn how they were going to do a massive stocktake and she was also going to learn the new stock systems which would soon be in place. It was all part of the changeover to the new large national chain to which they would now belong. Rebecca's manager had asked her to be responsible for the new stock systems as she needed to concentrate on the new till procedures and cash records.

Rebecca enjoyed the course and it was quite exciting being involved in all the activity that was going on. She was pleased that she had been chosen to take the additional responsibility and it meant that she would also have to train the other members of staff.

Rebecca realised that with the new sophisticated stock systems, they would be more efficient and therefore more profitable. The thought of redundancies seemed even less likely. It might even be that they would be so busy after the takeover that there would be opportunities for promotion for Rebecca as more staff were taken on!

Expanding the range

John was pleased when the branch of Off The Record started selling videos. Now that some of the groups were doing promotional videos it seemed a shame that they were missing out on sales. But Head Office had decided that they should be into 'home entertainment' which meant films too.

'Can I keep a record of sales in respect of the videos?' he asked Mr Gregory. 'Until we know a bit more about sales figures it is difficult to forecast how much stock we should be holding.'

'Yes please,' said Mr Gregory. 'You had better devise a system so that we know how many, what type, and any specialist requests we might get.'

New technology in the supermarket

Linda had been aware of the other supermarket in town getting a new type of till which read the bar code as you passed it through. No doubt they would be getting one soon.

'When will I be trained?' she asked. 'I only work at times when we are busy. That's what the part-timers are for. How can I possibly learn something like this when the place is full of customers?'

POINTS FOR DISCUSSION

1. Why do some people resist change. Make a list of the concerns some people have regarding change and then make a list of all the positive things about change.

2. If your store had the opportunity to take on a new range of goods, what might it be and how should it be dealt with?

3. Have you had to learn new skills? How was it dealt with in your store? Linda would need time to learn and practise with the new till before she would be confident to use it in a real life situation. Imagine you had to train someone to do something they had not done before. How would you go about it? Plan a training session and also decide how you could evaluate it and be sure that they were confident with their new skills.

TEST: DO YOU HAVE MANAGEMENT POTENTIAL?

Please don't look at this test until you are ready to take it. It will be challenging to you, and it is best if you do it when you have worked your way through the book, and have nearly completed your retail trading.

This test will simulate a demanding situation. You will need time to complete it. Set aside half a day for it, and make sure that nobody and nothing can disturb you.

If you complete the test thoroughly, using your retail experience, leadership skills, business instincts and common sense, you will find out if you've got what it takes for a career in retail management. Be completely honest. Nobody is going to see the results but you. By cheating you would only cheat yourself.

The situation

You are a trainee in a retail shop called Marcia's Boutique, which sells elegant ladies' clothes and fashion accessories. The shop is owned and run by Ms Marcia Millar.

It is winter, and there is a flu epidemic going round. It is a nasty type of flu, spreading quickly. Sufferers are ill for three weeks or more. Symptoms include fever, unbearable headaches, being unable to concentrate, and dizziness.

Several members of staff are already in bed with the flu and with strict doctor's orders not to get up.

It is Friday 2 pm, and on Monday the winter sales begin. This has always been the boutique's busiest and most profitable time.

The staff
The full complement of staff consists of:

- **You.** You have nearly completed your training. You possess a good general knowledge of fashion and of the way the shop is run. You know how to serve customers. During your training, you have been involved with administrative tasks, with buying and with stock control. But you have no idea about the financial side and haven't got a clue about how much money is in the bank account.

- Marcia Millar, the proprietor and manager. She left in the morning to go to London where her husband works. She was supposed to be back at noon, but she has not returned yet.

- The assistant manager, who is away on a luxury cruise with his wife. You know that he has won the prize in a magazine competition, that it is somewhere exotic, and that he will be away for two more weeks. You and your colleagues don't know the name of the ship, the cruise line, or the ports of call.

- The two senior sales assistants, who are in bed with flu and strict doctor's orders not to get up or go to work for at least ten days.

- A book keeper, who is so ill that she can't look after herself. She is staying with her parents, whose names, address or phone number nobody in the shop knows.

- A secretary who has been with the boutique for five years. She is not very bright, does not know anything about books or accounts and has no sales floor experience, but she is always willing to help, reliable, pleasant and friendly.

- A part-time sales assistant who also does the stock control. She has been with the boutique for fifteen years and thinks of herself as an 'old hand'. She is good at her job as long as everything happens at a slow pace and in an orderly fashion. However, she tends to respond to problems either by ignoring them and hoping they will go away, or by panicking and becoming hysterical. She lacks common sense and whenever something unexpected happens, she seems to make things worse.

- Three people who occasionally help in the shop on Saturdays: a student, a retiree, and a housewife. The housewife had been an assistant manager at a large grocer's shop before staying at home to look after her children. The student and the retiree have no retail training.

- A trainee who started training at the same time as you.

- A trainee who has been with the shop for two months only.

- An enthusiastic sixteen-year-old work-experience student in his second week, who is staying for another week.

The challenge

The phone rings. It is Mr Martin Millar, Marcia Millar's husband. He has devastating news.

'I'm phoning from the hospital. Marcia has had a serious accident. She's in intensive care. The doctors say she will probably be all right eventually, but only if we don't excite her in any way. They say I must not talk about business with her for at least a couple of weeks.

'I'm so glad that you are there. Only yesterday Marcia mentioned how much she values you. She has a high opinion of your skills and attitudes. Will you be able to run the shop, at least until the assistant manager comes back in a couple of weeks?'

'But – I'm only a trainee,' you manage to say.

'I am aware of this. But with all the senior staff away, you are the most experienced member of staff. And in this situation ability is more important than a formal qualification.'

You ask if he could not manage the shop. But he has a high-powered insurance job in London which he can't leave. Every spare minute he will spend at the hospital.

'Anyway, I know something about business, but nothing at all about retailing,' he says. 'Let's meet tonight at 7 pm. If you have an emergency plan prepared, we can discuss it.'

The complications

The part-time assistant – who has overheard the telephone conversation, says: 'You running the shop? That's nonsense. Of course I'm in charge. I have been with this shop longer than anyone else. I'm not going to let a trainee tell me what to do.'

The trainee who started at the same time as you and who has been sneezing all morning looks pale. She tries to hide the fact that she is taking aspirin. When you question her, she admits that she has a terrible headache as well as a sore throat, that she feels weak and dizzy. 'But don't worry, I'll manage. Normally, I would ask if I could go home. But not with everyone else off sick, and especially not now that you are in charge. I won't let you down. I'll battle on.'

You and the secretary look for the book-keeping and accounts documents, but you cannot find them. The secretary suggests the freelance accountant may have them.

The only people who are authorised to draw cheques from the business account are Ms Millar and the assistant manager.

Assignment 1
It is now 2 pm. This means you have three hours until many businesses (such as banks) close for the weekend, and five hours until the meeting with Mr Millar.

Write a 'to do' list of every action you are going to take during these hours.

Take your time over this assignment. Move on to the evaluation and to Assignment 2 only when you have completed Assignment 1.

Don't cheat – not even a glimpse at the evaluation is allowed.

Evaluation for Assignment 1
Compare your 'to do' list with the following list. For each item on this list which is included in your own list, give yourself one point.

- Inform the other members of staff of the accident.

- Hold an emergency meeting with members of staff, and ask them for their suggestions.

- Contact the three casual helpers and see if they are available for all, or part of the next two weeks.

- Ask the Saturday worker who has had a career in retailing if she could assist you in the running of the shop.

- Phone a recruitment agency (or several) and enquire about the rates and availability of temporary staff.

- Phone the local job centre.

- Phone the bank manager, explain the situation, and ask them to disclose the current bank balance (in view of the circumstances, they may give you this information even though you have no authorisation).

- Ask the bank manager if there is a way how you, or Mr Millar, or other members of staff could gain access to the money in the account should you need it.

- Phone the accountants to see if they have the books and financial documents, and if they remember what the financial situation was at the same time last year.

- Phone the local Chamber of Commerce to find out if they can give any advice.

- Phone the local Enterprise Agency for advice – they give free advice to small businesses.

- Talk to the managers of shops in the neighbourhood who may be able to give you advice.

- Send the colleague who is developing the flu symptoms home before she can spread the infection any further.

- Before she goes home, extract from her as much information as possible about anything useful she may know.

- Phone the two senior colleagues who are sick to see if they are able to give you some advice or information by phone.

- Consider ways in which you can protect both your own and your colleagues' health (vitamin pills, possibly flu vaccinations).

- See what can be done about mollifying the jealous part-time assistant – maybe give her special responsibility for a particular area.

- Invite the new trainee, the work-experience student and the secretary to a brief training session on how to serve customers, held by you on Sunday, but don't force them if they are unwilling.

- Delegate some of these jobs to other members of staff.

- Write out the requested emergency plan for Mr Millar with all your suggestions and queries.

- I have other useful 'to do' things on my list which are not included in the above.

> Number of points achieved in Assignment 1: _____

Assignment 2

Now write your report for Mr Millar. Imagine that this situation is real. Write the plan as if you were really going to hand it to him in the evening.

Include all your questions and requests, all your suggestions, and all the information he needs in order to make decisions about your suggestions, or which he may require during the next couple of weeks. For some suggestions, you may have to invent the information, *eg*, if the part-time staff are willing to work longer hours, or how much the going rates for temporary staff are. Use your imagination, but be realistic.

Please take your time in writing this plan, and consider every detail carefully. Look at the evaluation only after you have completed this assignment.

Evaluation 2

My report includes the following points (please tick and give yourself one point per tick).

- A request for a written authorisation. ____

- Details of what this authorisation should cover. ____

- A draft for the wording of the authorisation (for which you have obtained advice from the Chamber of Commerce, the Enterprise Agency or another source). ____

- A request that Mr Millar contacts key people *eg*, bank manager) who may be suspicious about a trainee who claims he/she is acting manager. ____

- A request that he confirms my appointment as acting manager to the other staff, especially the jealous part-time assistant. _____

- A request to keep in touch on a regular basis, *(eg* you or he phones every other day. _____

- A schedule of how many staff will be needed during the sales period. _____

- A schedule of when members of the full-time and part-time staff would be available. _____

- Information about the availability of temporary staff and the hourly or daily rates of pay. _____

- The estimated cost of taking on extra staff during the period. _____

- Suggestions for giving quick customer-care training to the secretary, the new trainee and the work-experience person. _____

- Expected problems relating to your authority, *eg* from the jealous part-time assistant. _____

- The current financial situation as far as you have been able to ascertain. _____

- Suggestions for how to access the bank account if necessary (following the bank manager's advice) or other solutions. _____

- Plans for ordering/reordering stock. _____

- An estimate of the daily takings during the sales period. _____

- Whether a cash flow problem is anticipated and if so, when. _____

- A list of staff home telephone numbers (as far as available). _____

- A list of other useful/relevant contact names and phone numbers, *eg* bank manager, accountant, recruitment agency. _____

- I have at least one other point on my list which I think is relevant but is not listed here. _____

- I have produced this report in duplicate: one copy for Mr Millar, one for me. _____

| Number of points achieved in Assignment 2: | ____ |

Assignment 3

Evaluation of the assignment
Tick every statement which applies to you, as many as applicable.

- I found this test

enjoyable	____	(B)
challenging	____	(B)
exciting	____	(B)
too much work	____	(C)
interesting	____	(B)
complicated	____	(A)
confusing	____	(C)
timeconsuming	____	(A)
tiring	____	(C)
boring	____	(C)
stimulating	____	(B)
difficult	____	(A)

- I wrote down some notes and thoughts, but I didn't produce a full well-presented report. ____ (A)

- I took care with the presentation of the report, and I tried to make it look complete and professional. ____ (B)

- I gave some thought to the questions, but I didn't
  have the time to write a report.   ____ (C)

- In such a situation I would be (tick as many as applicable)

nervous	____ (A)
proud	____ (B)
ambitious	____ (B)
annoyed	____ (C)
frightened	____ (C)
panicking	____ (C)
excited	____ (B)
worried	____ (A)
feeling the first flu symptoms	____ (C)
full of energy	____ (B)
challenged	____ (B)

How would you cope?

If such a situation happened to me, I would (tick one of the following statements; the letters in brackets will tell you how you score at the end):

- Accept the responsibility and enjoy the challenge.   ____ (B)

- Be a bit apprehensive, but make the best of it.   ____ (B)

- Suggest to Mr Millar to close the shop for two weeks.   ____ (C)

- Admit honestly that I don't have the experience and
  skills required to manage a shop yet.   ____ (A)

- Leave the running of the shop to the jealous
  part-time assistant.   ____ (C)

- Suggest to Mr Millar that the Saturday helper
  who used to be an assistant manager takes over
  the management.   ____ (A)

- Pretend that I've got the flu.   ____ (C)

What makes a good retail manager?
Tick the *five* criteria which you think are the most important.

Someone who:

- is good at dealing with people generally ____ (B)
- always knows the right answer ____ (C)
- has influence in high places ____ (C)
- always has time for everyone ____ (A)
- is well organised ____ (B)
- has a superior education, e.g. a university degree ____ (C)
- can set and achieve targets ____ (B)
- keeps calm under pressure ____ (B)
- is quick at making decisions ____ (A)
- always sticks to his/her plans whatever happens ____ (C)
- is ambitious ____ (A)
- is always learning new retail or management related skills ____ (B)
- makes him/herself indispensible everywhere ____ (C)
- has a good head for figures ____ (A)
- is highly respected by the staff ____ (A)
- can impose his/her will on others. ____ (C)

Total your scores
Evaluation of Assignment 3:
Number of 'A's ticked: ____
Number of 'B's ticked: ____
Number of 'C's ticked: ____

Give yourself one point for every B ticked. Deduct one point for every C ticked (even if you end up with a minus number). The As don't count anything.

Total number of points achieved in Assignment 3: ____

Final test evaluation
Add up the number of points achieved in assignments 1, 2 and 3.

Total points achieved: _____

0–4
This result is not very impressive. It seems that retailing is not the right career for you. Consider taking your skills elsewhere, and choosing a career which suits your personal talents and interests better. On the other hand, maybe you have simply rushed through the tasks without thinking properly. Remember that all important and difficult situations require time and thought.

5–10
You are good at your job. You prefer regular work hours, and a pleasant, peaceful environment. You don't want to take more stress or responsibility than is absolutely necessary. You are happier if someone else deals with any problems arising, and takes the decisions. You are not particularly ambitious. However, you are thorough, reliable, willing and helpful – the fact that you have completed this test proves it. Every shop needs people like you.

11–24
You are the type who will make a good manager, but you are not ready for it yet. The potential is there, but first you need more experience in the retail world and more confidence in yourself. In a few years, you will be ready to move up the ladder, and you will be good at it. In the meantime, try to find a job in retailing which offers variety and suits your personal interests.

25–43
Very well done! Your result is better than one would expect from a trainee. You definitely have the potential for a retail manager, and you will enjoy the career. Start now exploring what options you have for further development, either within the company or elsewhere, but don't rush your decisions. Aim for a career in a retail sector in which you are particularly interested. Enquire about in-house training and staff development.

More than 43
Congratulations! You are a natural manager. In fact, your result is suspiciously good for a trainee. You haven't cheated, have you? Or are you already a manager who is doing this test just out of curiosity?

You handled the simulated situation exceptionally well, and you understand what it takes to be a good manager. You are thorough, methodical, well organised, quick at grasping situations and able to adapt to changes and deal with surprises.

Have you planned your career yet? Set yourself ambitious targets, and you will thrive on them. Let your employers know about your ambitions. If there are no prospects for development within the store where you are working, look out for opportunities elsewhere. Otherwise you will get bored quickly.

If there isn't a chance for early promotion within your company, and you cannot find a job with better prospects elsewhere, consider attending management training courses in your spare time. Such courses are often organised by the local adult education centres or chambers of commerce. When the right opening comes, you'll have the skills for it.

National Vocational Qualifications

National Vocational Qualifications (NVQs) in Retailing are available at Levels 1, 2, 3 and 4. They are nationally recognised qualifications which are transferable from one employer to another.

- **Level 1** is appropriate to a junior sales assistant who carries out routine tasks, safely and effectively and does not make decisions or has any level of responsibility.

- **Level 2** would be the qualification of a sales assistant who will carry out more varied tasks and will have a certain amount of personal autonomy. They manage their own time and make some decisions about how a job is carried out.

- **Level 3** is appropriate for someone who has responsibility for making decisions about work and other members of staff. They carry out a range of duties under a variety of different circumstances. They contribute to the control of budgets and contribute to policy-making decisions.

- **Level 4** is a member of management who has responsibilities for the recruitment and development of staff, budgets, operational procedures and policy-making decisions.

NVQ Retailing
Level 2

Level 2 is based on ten compulsary units plus at least two optional units from the list, as follows:

Compulsory units

Providing a service to the customer	See chapter 2
Contributing to the maintenance of health and safety	See chapter 6
Contributing to good housekeeping routines	See chapter 9
Maintaining relationships in the workplace	See chapter 8
Contributing to the security of the workplace	See chapter 7
Handling stock	See chapters 10 & 11
Processing the sale	See chapter 4
Contributing to communications within the organisation	See chapter 8
Dealing with returned goods and complaints	See chapter 5
Displaying and merchandising stock	See chapter 3

Optional units

Achieving a sale	See chapter 2
Maintaining hygienic standards of food handling	See chapter 11
Completing sales administration	
Maintaining stock records	

Dealing with prescriptions and medicines

Organising repair or service of goods

Supplying tools/equipment for hire

Handling machinery

Dealing with orders

Recording sales transactions

Dealing with home news deliveries

Creating and maintaining a database of information

You may be surprised to see 'Achieving a Sale' as an optional unit when it could be said that anyone who works in retail would be involved in achieving a sale. Linda at Westmore's Supermarket would be involved in taking the money and providing service at the till-point but she would not be able to influence the customer's choice or use any selling skills in the same way that a furniture salesperson might. So if this unit appeared in the compulsory list, Linda would not be able to achieve the qualification.

How you can find out more about NVQs
There are several people or organisations who can tell you more about NVQs. These are:

- your employer or the company's personnel department
- your trade union representative
- your local further education college
- your local Jobcentre
- your local Training and Enterprise Council (TEC)
- Customer Services, NCVQ, 222 Euston Road, London NW1 2BZ Tel: (0171) 728 1914.

Glossary

Bar code. The series of vertical black lines which can be read by a decoder and transcribed into stock information.

Cash equivalents. Anything that takes the place of cash – this could be credit cards, debit cards, cheques, coupons or vouchers.

EPOS. Electronic Point of Sale – a computerised till which records credit card transactions. It can also record stock details, operator details, time and other relevant information.

Features & benefits. Characteristics of the item which will be appealing to the customer.

Imprinter. The machine which imprints details of credit cards on to handwritten vouchers.

Merchandising. Displaying the correct amount of stock, in the correct place, according to potential sales based on sales forecasts.

Reduce down. Taking some stock off sale when the line is not selling in order to make space for stock which is more likely to sell.

Replenishing. Filling up shelves/rails to replace stock that has been sold.

Sell-by date. The recommended date by which the item should be sold if the item is perishable.

Sew-in label. The label inside a garment which will show size, washing instructions, fabric content and country of origin.

Stock rotation. Placing the older stock at the front of the shelves/racks so that it sells first.

Swiping. The process of running a credit card between two metal runners which will read the magnetic information on the credit card.

Voids. The result of an error being made which has to be reversed.

Useful Addresses

ORGANISATIONS TO WRITE TO REGARDING MANAGEMENT TRAINING SCHEMES

Harrods Limited, Recruitment Department, Knightsbridge, London SW1X 7XL. Tel: (0171) 730 1234.

Selfridges Limited, 400 Oxford Street, London W1A 1AB. Tel: (0171) 629 1234.

John Lewis plc, The Administration Manager (for graduate recruitment only), Personnel DS, 171 Victoria Street, London SW1E 5NN. Tel: (0171) 828 1000.

John Lewis plc, The Deputy Staff Manager (for A level and other recruitment), 278/306 Oxford Street, London W1A 1EX. Tel: (0171) 629 7711.

The Burton Group (includes Dorothy Perkins, Principles, Top Shop/Man, Debenhams and Evans), Personnel Department, 214 Oxford Street, London W1N 9DF. Tel: (0171) 636 8040.

W. H. Smith Limited, Graduate Recruitment, Milton Hill House, Milton Hill, Abingdon, Oxfordshire OX13 6AS. Tel: (01235) 831474.

Marks and Spencer plc, Michael House, Baker Street, London W1A 1DN. Tel: (0171) 935 4422.

Boots the Chemist, Graduate Recruitment, 1 Thane Road West, Nottingham NG2 3AA. Tel: (0115) 950 6111.

B&Q plc, Portswood House, 1 Hampshire Corporate Park, Chandlers Ford, Hants SO53 3YX. Tel: (01703) 256256.

BhS plc, Marylebone House, 129–137 Marylebone Road, London NW1 5QD. Tel: (0171) 262 3288.

J Sainsbury plc, The Graduate Recruitment Department, Stamford House, Stamford Street, London SE1 9LL. Tel: (0171) 921 6000.

Safeway plc, Personnel Department, 6 Millington Road, Hayes, Middlesex. Tel: (0181) 848 8744.

Tesco Stores Limited, PO Box 18, Delamare Road, Cheshunt, Waltham Cross, Herts EN8 9SL. Tel: (01992) 632222.

Further Reading

TRADE JOURNALS

The Retail Pocket Book.
Retail Review.
Retail Week.
Retail World.
Drapers Record.

LIBRARY BOOKS

The Shopkeeper's Handbook, P. Levene (Graham & Trotman, 1989)
Retailing, Gerald Pintel and Jay Diamond (Prentice-Hall, 1983)
Training for Selling, Distributive Trades EDC (HMSO, 1971)

DEVELOPING YOUR WORK SKILLS

How to Communicate at Work, Ann Dobson (How To Books, 1994)
How To Manage People at Work, John Humphries (How To Books, 2nd edition, 1995)
How To Write a CV That Works, Paul McGee (How To Books, 1995)
How To Market Yourself, Ian Phillipson (How To Books, 1995)
How To Know Your Rights at Work, Robert Spicer (How To Books, 2nd edition 1995)
How To Master Business English, Michael Bennie (How To Books, 2nd edition, 1994)

Index